Pied-á-Terre

by

John S. Anastasi

FOUNDED 1830

NEW YORK HOLLYWOOD LONDON TORONTO

SAMUELFRENCH.COM

Copyright © 2008 by John S. Anastasi
ALL RIGHTS RESERVED

CAUTION: Professionals and amateurs are hereby warned that PIED-Á-TERRE is subject to a royalty. It is fully protected under the copyright laws of the United States of America, the British Commonwealth, including Canada, and all other countries of the Copyright Union. All rights, including professional, amateur, motion picture, recitation, lecturing, public reading, radio broadcasting, television and the rights of translation into foreign languages are strictly reserved. In its present form the play is dedicated to the reading public only.

The amateur live stage performance rights to PIED-Á-TERRE are controlled exclusively by Samuel French, Inc., and royalty arrangements and licenses must be secured well in advance of presentation. PLEASE NOTE that amateur royalty fees are set upon application in accordance with your producing circumstances. When applying for a royalty quotation and license please give us the number of performances intended, dates of production, your seating capacity and admission fee. Royalties are payable one week before the opening performance of the play to Samuel French, Inc., at 45 W. 25th Street, New York, NY 10010 or to Samuel French (Canada), Ltd., 100 Lombard Street, Lower Level, Toronto, Ontario, Canada M5C 1M3.

Royalty of the required amount must be paid whether the play is presented for charity or gain and whether or not admission is charged.

Stock royalty quoted upon application to Samuel French, Inc.

For all other rights than those stipulated above, apply to: Mid life Crisis Productions, 264 Scenic Pine Drive, Hollidaysburg, PA 16648.

Particular emphasis is laid on the question of amateur or professional readings, permission and terms for which must be secured in writing from Samuel French, Inc.

Copying from this book in whole or in part is strictly forbidden by law, and the right of performance is not transferable.

Whenever the play is produced the following notice must appear on all programs, printing and advertising for the play: "Produced by special arrangement with Samuel French, Inc."

Due authorship credit must be given on all programs, printing and advertising for the play.

ISBN 978-0-573-65241-7   Printed in U.S.A.   #17814

No one shall commit or authorize any act or omission by which the copyright of, or the right to copyright, this play may be impaired.

No one shall make any changes in this play for the purpose of production.

Publication of this play does not imply availability for performance. Both amateurs and professionals considering a production are strongly advised in their own interests to apply to Samuel French, Inc., for written permission before starting rehearsals, advertising, or booking a theatre.

No part of this book may be reproduced, stored in a retrieval system, or transmitted in any form, by any means, now known or yet to be invented, including mechanical, electronic, photocopying, recording, videotaping, or otherwise, without the prior written permission of the publisher.

IMPORTANT BILLING AND CREDIT REQUIREMENTS

All producers of PIED-Á-TERRE *must* give credit to the Author of the Play in all programs distributed in connection with performances of the Play, and in all instances in which the title of the Play appears for the purposes of advertising, publicizing or otherwise exploiting the Play and/or a production. The name of the Author *must* appear on a separate line on which no other name appears, immediately following the title and *must* appear in size of type not less than fifty percent of the size of the title type.

PIED-À-TERRE was originally developed and produced by Mid Life Crisis Productions, Inc. in a showcase production at the Beckett Theater at Theatre Row in September 2004 under the direction of Mitch Poulos with the following cast and creative staff:

JACK . . . . Patrick Johnson
JULIA . . . . Susan Estes
KATIE . . . . Valerie Blazak

Set Design: Cindy Bennett
Lightening Design: Mark Hankla
Sound Design: Mitch Poulos
Casting: Roxy Horen
General Manager: Paul Morer Productions
Stage Manager: Parys Le Bron

PIED-À-TERRE was initially presented as a stage reading as part of the TRU (Theatre Resources Unlimited) New Play Reading Series 2005 produced by Jared Cohen at the Players Theater under the direction of Bradlee Bing with the following cast:

JACK . . . . Jim DePavia
JULIA . . . . Hilary Smith
KATIE . . . . Ryman Sneed

PIED-À-TERRE was first produced at Penn State University in August of 2006 with the following cast:

JACK . . . . Jim DePavia
JULIA . . . . Sonja Stuart
KATIE . . . . Christine Ryndak

Director: Bradlee Bing
Set Design: Randall Parsons
Casting: Barry Moss Casting
General Manager: The Splinter Group

Produced by Jeff Britton and Broadway Bound Productions in association with Bob Ost and Theatre Resources Unlimited.

PIED-À-TERRE received its New York Off Broadway world premier on December 1, 2007 at the Kirk Theater at Theater Row. Produced by Stageplays Theatre Company (Stageplays®) under the direction of Tom Ferriter with the following cast and creative staff:

JACK . . . . John Howard Swain
JULIA . . . . Robin Riker
KATIE . . . . Jessica McKee

Set Design: Randall Parsons
Costume Design: Brad Scoggins
Sound Design: Chris Rummel
Light Design: Jeff Koger
Original Music: Michael Valenti
Choreography: Ron De Jesus
Casting Director: Laura Dragomir
Stage Manager: Cheryl D. Olszowka, assisted by Danielle Teague-Daniels.

CHARACTERS

JULIA, Late forties, professional newscaster
KATIE, Nineteen year old streetwise woman
JACK, Fifties, lawyer

TIME AND PLACE

The time is current. The action takes place over a year period in an elegant Manhattan apartment.

ACT I
Scene One: Present time
Scene Two: Six months earlier
Scene Three: Present time
Scene Four: Four months earlier
Scene Five: Present time

ACT II
Scene One: Present time
Scene Two: Two weeks earlier
Scene Three: Present time
Scene Four: One year earlier merging with present time

For my Father
"My life has been a poor attempt to imitate the man…"

ACT I

Scene I

Setting: Upper East Side Manhattan apartment. Present time.

(*As the lights come up,* **JULIA** *cautiously enters the apartment. She pauses at the carousel. Almost reverently, she turns it on. She crosses to the desk. She picks up a sealed, unaddressed greeting card and begins to open it. The phone rings, startling her. She drops the card and picks up the phone.*)

JULIA. (*on phone*) Hello. (*pause*) Who? Cellini's. Jack Davis. Yes…and that was for three at eight tonight? No. I'll be cancelling that. Yes, thank you.

(*She hangs up the phone and returns it to the base on the desk. She notices a small recorder. She is affected by the familiar voice.*)

JACK'S VOICE. Susan again, page 14, Section 2 (*pause*) yes, page 15, Section 2…check your book! The execution and delivery of this agreement by each of the parties. Susan, it's called Maid For You in New York. This place really needs it.

(**JULIA** *turns and enters the master bedroom. The door to the apartment opens.* **KATIE** *hurriedly enters. She wears head phones and carries the distinctive shopping bag from Victoria's Secret, and a backpack.* **JULIA** *enters the room. Surprised, they scream.*)

KATIE. Oh shit! You scared me. I wasn't expecting anyone. (*beat*) Oh, are you the cleaning lady?

JULIA. (*barely able to speak*) Who…who…who –

KATIE. (*trying to speak Spanish*) Cleano el apartmento?

JULIA. I speak English. Who are –

KATIE. Great! Jack mentioned you were coming; I totally forgot.

(**KATIE** *opens the Victoria's Secret bag and pulls out a piece of clothing.*)

Hey, I know it's not part of your job, but can you help me?

(*She holds up a silk, slinky negligee.*)

Tell me what you think? Today's our anniversary. I got a big surprise for him. Do you think Jack will like it?

JULIA. (*shocked*) Wow.

KATIE. Too much, huh? I told that girl it was...overstated. Shit, I don't want to turn him off. Damn...maybe something less obvious...or, or *inconspicuous*. Yeah, that's it... *inconspicuous*. I wonder if I got anything in the closet.

(**KATIE** *runs into the guest bedroom with the nightgown. After a few moments, she returns.*)

Okay, I'm all right. I'll bring it out only if I need the big guns.

(**KATIE** *reaches in her pants and pulls out a pack of gum. She chews rather obviously but not obnoxiously.*)

JULIA. You know Jack?

KATIE. Look, it would be great if you could finish up as soon as you can. He's going to be home soon and I want everything to be perfect. God, I love my place. Look at this view.

JULIA. You actually live here?

KATIE. I do now. It beats the crap holes I was living in.
Shit, I got to get moving!

(**KATIE** *smacks her face.*)

Damn you, potty mouth!

(*She runs into the bedroom.* **JULIA** *crosses to the couch and starts to pick up Katie's backpack.* **KATIE** *enters.*)

Forgot *my* stuff. (*beat*) You're not cleaning.

(**KATIE** *crosses to her and takes her backpack.*)

JULIA. I'm not cleaning.

KATIE. Then, what are you doing here? (*pause*) Who are you?

(*A moment as* **JULIA** *considers.*)

JULIA. Jack's slightly embarrassed…sister.

KATIE. His sister?

JULIA. Yes, he gave me a key sometime ago and told me I could use the place when I was in New York. I had no idea he was –

KATIE. You're his sister! Oh my God. I've never met any of the family. I'm Katie McDaniels. A sheer delectation.

(**KATIE** *crosses and gives her a big hug.* **JULIA** *steps back, stunned.*)

JULIA. (*utter disbelief*) I didn't expect anyone to be here.

KATIE. I moved in about five months ago. Before that, it was a different place every month, but they were all… terrible, or…let's see…ah…*hideous*, that's it, *hideous*. Not like here.

(*As* **KATIE** *speaks she crosses to a painting on the wall. She proudly straightens the painting.*)

Do you like this painting?

JULIA. Not especially.

KATIE. I picked this one out, or rather, "it called to me". The mood…I know what they're feeling. Jack really loves it.

JULIA. It doesn't look like the type of art he –

KATIE. He loves my taste. Jack says that when I get done with my degree I can be a famous interior decorator. He's so…*insistent* about college…like it's the be all and end all. He won't get off it. So I humor him. But this is what I really want to do. Pick out and hang the…the… *pulchritudinous* things that I can't afford.

JULIA. How long have you known him?

KATIE. Six months ago today. He didn't tell you about me?

(**JULIA** *shakes her head.*)

We met at the Eighth Avenue Food Emporium. It was so romantic.

JULIA. (*in disbelief*) You met at a grocery store? Jack was shopping? (*beat*) For food?

KATIE. He always does the shopping.

JULIA. Christ! (*beat*) You fell in love at the deli counter?

KATIE. No silly...on line.

JULIA. The internet?

KATIE. The checkout line.

JULIA. Oh.

KATIE. Friday after midnight. That's *always* my shopping time. You know, I worked real late, and I can never get out of bed in the morning except for mass on Sunday, so it's the best time for me to grocery shop, and 'cause you don't got to fight the crowds.

JULIA. Uh-huh.

KATIE. So I'm in line, and the guy is checking off my stuff, and what do you know, I'm like seven bucks short. Has that ever happened to you?

JULIA. (*hesitantly*) No.

KATIE. I wanted...to die. So I'm standing there, and he tells me I have to put some food back. I'm...I'm...*dismayed.* So I pull the stuff out of the bag and I'm trying to figure out what I really don't need...the BumbleBee Tuna fish, or Campbell's Chicken Noodle Soup, or my One-a-Day Vitamins and I'm adding the stuff up in my head and –

JULIA. Jack leaned over and paid for the food.

KATIE. (*surprised*) You really know your brother.

JULIA. Apparently that's his M.O.

(**KATIE** *looks confused*)

Modus operandi?

KATIE. Whatever. Out of no where, this guy...this prince in a black tuxedo slaps a fifty on the counter and tells the clerk to put all the stuff back in the bag.

JULIA. That's Jack all right.

KATIE. Oh, I know. I looked at him, he looked at me and by the time we got the bags in the cart...hell, I was in love.

(*A moment.*)

JULIA. You don't find it a little...how would *you* say it... *idiosyncratic?*

KATIE. What?

JULIA. The age difference. I mean, he's fifty...you're –

KATIE. Nineteen.

JULIA. (*to herself*) Jesus Christ!

KATIE. It's cool. I really don't like guys my age. They're so... so...infantile. Not like Jack. He knows how to treat a woman. He respects me.

JULIA. (*in pain*) Oh...

(**JULIA** *sits down and holds her stomach.*)

KATIE. Damn, you don't look great. Can I get you something?

JULIA. My gastritis is acting up. Do you have any Tums?

KATIE. I think we have something in the kitchen. I'll take a look.

(**KATIE** *crosses to the kitchen.*)

(O.S.) I had a friend who looked like that once.

(**KATIE** *sticks her head out of the kitchen shutters.*)

(*whispering*) She had cancer.

JULIA. I don't have cancer.

KATIE. (O.S.) It's okay if you did. I mean, they have great treatments now.

JULIA. That's comforting. (*beat*) How would you know?

(**KATIE** *enters and hands* **JULIA** *the Tums.*)

KATIE. Jack told me.

JULIA. You talk medicine with him?

KATIE. We talk everything. Any subject. He's...(*proudly*) *coruscating*.

JULIA. Why do you do that?

KATIE. Do what?

JULIA. Speak like your brain is attached to a thesaurus.

KATIE. It makes me sound smarter.

JULIA. I see.

   (*Uncomfortable moment.*)

KATIE. You have any kids?

   (**JULIA** *starts to speak, then hesitates.*)

   I bet they know all the right words to use. Not like me.

   (**JULIA** *turns from her.*)

   Oh, I'm sorry.

JULIA. What for?

KATIE. Your kids are as dumb as I am.

   (**JULIA** *stands and reels defensively.*)

JULIA. (*proudly*) Laura is a freshman at Stanford. Full academic scholarship.

KATIE. Wow.

JULIA. Yes...wow. My Laura sounds and even *looks* very intelligent.

   (*A moment as* **JULIA** *studies* **KATIE** *chewing.*)

KATIE. What?

JULIA. Do you enjoy that as much as it appears?

KATIE. (*beat*) Oh...the gum. You should have seen me before. Jack really hated it. I only chew one piece at a time now; it's more lady like.

JULIA. He told you that?

KATIE. He spends a lot of time teaching me stuff. I guess he wants someone to talk to...after.

JULIA. After what?

KATIE. You know.

   (**KATIE** *winks at her.* **JULIA** *grabs her stomach.*)

JULIA. Oh shit.

KATIE. More cramps? That could be a ruptured cyst. I had –

JULIA. I'm fine.

(*A moment.*)

KATIE. Are you his big sister or his little sister?

JULIA. I feel pretty little right now.

KATIE. Jack told me about his brother but not you. Aren't you guys close?

JULIA. Not as close as I thought.

KATIE. You're pretty shocked, huh?

JULIA. He's never mentioned you.

KATIE. Oh, that is strange. (*beat*) Are you and the wife tight?

JULIA. The wife. The wife! He told you he was married?

KATIE. We have no secrets.

JULIA. What did he tell you about her?

KATIE. Everything. That she's pretty smart, and I think she's on some TV show –

JULIA. (*proudly*) She's an anchor woman for WTNH. (*beat*) Channel 8 in Connecticut.

KATIE. Never saw it. (*beat*) Oh shit, I just realized something. (*beat*) She's your sister-in-law.

JULIA. Yes.

KATIE. I guess that makes me...the enemy?

JULIA. Not necessarily.

KATIE. But she's your relative.

JULIA. She is, but frankly, I never really liked her.

(**KATIE** *crosses and sits with her on the couch.*)

KATIE. I just...*empatize* with him.

JULIA. Empathize?

KATIE. That's what I said. You know, 'cause the way she is.

JULIA. And how is she?

KATIE. Way different from me.

JULIA. (*smirking*) Yes. (*beat*) How so?

KATIE. "I'm the microwave, and his wife's the freezer."

(*A moment.*)

JULIA. (*shocked and hurt*) He actually told you that?

(**KATIE** *laughs to herself.*)

KATIE. No, not in those words. She's real emotionally detached. I'm not supposed to talk about it. I guess it was *lucky* for me though.

JULIA. Why lucky?

KATIE. Well, if he got what he *needed* from her, I wouldn't be here, would I?

JULIA. You're asking *me*? (*beat*) Right now, I'm the last person that could explain my...my brother's *needs*.

(**KATIE** *crosses to the carousel.*)

KATIE. Tonight...tonight. It's so exciting. He's giving me a gift. You know what that means?

JULIA. God only knows.

(**KATIE** *extends her left hand and looks at her ring finger.*)

KATIE. Oh come on. Two people, in love...it's a natural course of events. He's going to pop the question.

(**KATIE** *begins to turn the carousel.* **JULIA** *aggressively protects it.* **KATIE** *steps back*)

It's okay. I think Jack fixed it.

JULIA. (*strongly*) It was *never* broken. (*beat*) You've *only* known him for six months.

KATIE. It could be six days...or six hours. With Jack, it's so easy. Being here, with him...it just feels right. (*beat*) This is great.

JULIA. What is?

KATIE. To have someone to talk to about Jack. I haven't got any real friends and you can fill me in on the first fifty years. I want to know...I want to be...everything in his life. I have to make this happen. He's ready, and I'm so ready I'm going to burst.

JULIA. Nineteen. Surely your parents aren't happy about this?

KATIE. Nothing I ever did made Dad happy. And Mom, well I think she would have liked Jack. At least on the days she was conscious.

JULIA. Was she ill?

KATIE. No. She drank till she passed out.

JULIA. (*sarcastically*) I'm sure that made it hard for her to be a good mother.

KATIE. (*defensively*) She was a *great* mother. But, the more drunk she was the less she had to hear from good old Pop. Controlling, disapproving prick. (*beat*) I didn't want to leave her but I knew I would just die if I stayed at home one more day. The night I left I went back into my mom's bedroom and whispered in her ear that I would be back to take care of her – to get her away from him.

JULIA. You do know that he has children?

KATIE. Had. He told me about Sarah. That was pretty sad.

JULIA. That *was* pretty sad.

KATIE. Oh, I'm sorry. She was your niece.

JULIA. Yes.

(*Uncomfortable moment.*)

KATIE. Will you excuse me? I need to use the bathroom.

(**KATIE** *crosses to the guest bedroom.* **JULIA** *slowly moves about the room and sits at the piano. She picks up several pages of sheet music.*)

JULIA. (*to herself*) Jack Davis Opus 1. He actually finished it!

(*The music of Jack's Opus 1 begins as the lights fade to black.* **JULIA** *exits in the darkness. Katie's painting is now replaced with another piece of art work. After a few moments, the lights resume.*)

Scene II

Setting: The apartment. Six months earlier.

(**JACK**, *dressed in a formal black tuxedo, quickly enters from the master bedroom. He nervously adjusts the lights, straightens the pillows on the couch, and crosses to the piano and sits. He struggles to play Beethoven's Opus 28 as he frequently gazes towards the guest bedroom. After a few moments* **KATIE** *enters from the bathroom. She is provocatively dressed. She chews gum obnoxiously and has a tough demeanor. She stands and listens for a few moments.*)

KATIE. That's nice shit.

JACK. Thank you…I think. It's getting there. Do you like Beethoven?

KATIE. I don't know. Did I ever fuck him?

(**JACK** *stops playing.*)

JACK. I doubt it.

KATIE. Don't. I've been on my back for months now.

JACK. He's been dead for a hundred and eighty years.

KATIE. So have some of the perverts I've been with.

JACK. Would you like a soda?

KATIE. I'll take a beer.

JACK. There's no alcohol in this apartment. 7UP or Coke?

(**JACK** *exits to the kitchen.*)

KATIE. 7UP. (*beat*) Bring the can!

(**KATIE** *crosses and looks at the carousel.*)

You don't drink?

JACK (O.S.). Special occasions only.

(**JACK** *enters carrying a glass.*)

Don't smoke either.

KATIE. (*sarcastic*) Exciting guy.

JACK. Just careful. (*beat*) I assume you're not of drinking age.

KATIE. I'm nineteen.

JACK. It's twenty-one in New York.

KATIE. So what are you...a cop?

JACK. No, a lawyer.

KATIE. Hooking is illegal, too.

JACK. Here.

(**JACK** *hands the glass to her. She doesn't take it.*)

KATIE. Where is it?

JACK. What?

KATIE. The can?

JACK. I threw it out.

KATIE. You take a swig first.

JACK. I'm a coffee addict. (*beat*) Don't trust me?

KATIE. (*imitating Jack*) Just careful.

(**JACK** *takes the glass, sips the soda, and hands it back to* **KATIE.** **KATIE** *removes the large wad of gum from her mouth and sticks it on the side of the glass. She chugs the soda, puts the empty glass down, and puts the gum back in her mouth. She crosses to* **JACK**, *drops to her knees, and starts to unbuttons his pants.*)

JACK. What are you doing?

KATIE. What you paid me for.

JACK. Let's talk for a while?

(**KATIE** *crosses to the chair and sits.*)

KATIE. It's your hour.

(*A moment.*)

JACK. Serena? That's a pretty name. Where did that come from?

KATIE. My mother. She said when I was born I was exotic looking. An exotic baby needed an exotic name. (*beat*) Serena.

JACK. Funny, the name is slightly incongruent to your habit.

KATIE. What's incongruent? I mean just in case there's

someone else here who doesn't know what it means.

JACK. Doesn't go with...doesn't match.

KATIE. Oh. (*beat*) What habit?

JACK. The chewing of that large wad of gum in your mouth. How many pieces do you have in there?

KATIE. (*calculating*) Maybe...eight.

JACK. Your dentist must be thrilled.

KATIE. It's been a long night.

(**JACK** *picks up a glass ashtray and places it under her chin.* **KATIE** *drops open her mouth and the big wad of gum falls into the ashtray.*)

I thought you didn't smoke?

JACK. I don't.

(**KATIE** *stares at the ashtray.*)

Oh, it's been in my life since I was ten. Always sat on the coffee table next to the couch. My father had this talent of peeling an apple in one continuous piece. He would leave the peels in the ashtray, and I would race over and eat –

KATIE. Too much information.

(*A moment*)

JACK. How did you get into this type of work?

KATIE. You aren't going to try to save me, are you?

JACK. No. I was just interested –

KATIE. (*sarcastically*) It was my major in college. (*beat*) I have a masters in Fuckology and a minor in Blowjobmatics.

JACK. You could do better.

KATIE. Yeah, I could discover the cure to Cirrhosis.

(**JACK**, *surprised, looks at her for a moment.*)

JACK. Well, that's pretty specific, but it's possible. The moment you commit is when the world comes into sync with you. Reach for the stars.

KATIE. (*sarcastically*) Wow, that's deep. (*beat*) I make enough money to care for myself. I'm doing fine.

JACK. Fine? You offered me...fellatio in front of the Food

Emporium.

KATIE. So what?

JACK. Well, it's not the usual career path a young woman chooses –

(**KATIE** *glares at him and crosses to the door.*)

KATIE. I'm out of here.

JACK. If you do so well...why don't you have your own place?

KATIE. That's freaky. How would you know that?

(**JACK** *quickly tries to recover.*)

JACK. I just assumed –

KATIE. Well don't!

JACK. Where do you live?

KATIE. You're not paying me for personal information.

JACK. You'll have sex with me, but you won't tell me where you live?

(**KATIE** *ponders, then delivers a rote speech.*)

KATIE. I moved out of my parents home fifteen months ago. I was living at my boyfriend's place, but then we broke up. I've been jumping between friends' apartments till I find a place of my own.

JACK. I see.

(*Uncomfortable silence.*)

KATIE. Do you always pick up girls, dressed like a penguin?

JACK. Not usually.

KATIE. Where were you tonight?

JACK. *Coppelia.* (*beat*) The ballet. I'm a large contributor.

KATIE. Was it good?

JACK. I don't know.

KATIE. Didn't you watch it?

(**KATIE** *awkwardly and subconsciously moves into first position.*)

JACK. Yes and no. (*beat*) I found it hard to concentrate

tonight.
Do you like the ballet?

(**KATIE** *quickly recovers and breaks out of position.*)

KATIE. Barbie liked it.

JACK. Barbie?

KATIE. Barbie. You know, Barbie and fucking Ken? I used to dress her up as a prima ballerina and dance all over my room.

JACK. Sounds fun.

KATIE. It was better than our family bonding time.

(*A moment.*)

JACK. Have you ever seen one?

KATIE. (*sadly*) Ballet wasn't part of the "plan" for me.

JACK. Maybe I can take you.

(**KATIE** *looks at her watch.*)

KATIE. You're down to a half hour, Romeo.

JACK. I need to get out of this "bird suit." Make yourself comfortable.

KATIE. Hey, it's your money, but minutes are ticking away and you're not getting laid.

(**JACK** *exits to the bedroom.* **KATIE** *turns and looks at the impressive library.*)

All these books yours?

JACK (O.S.). Every one.

(*She takes one off of the bookshelf and reads the inside cover.*)

KATIE. You read them all?

JACK (O.S.). Nobody reads them all. (*beat*) I'm getting to them. One at a time.

KATIE. (*to herself, looking through the books*) Let's see what he's got here. Boring, boring, can't pronounce it...okay, here's a big mother.

(*She takes a book off the shelf and reads the title.*)

The Da Capo Catalog of Classical Music Compositions.

(*She reads the inscription in the book.*)

To Jack. It's our dreams that make this life tolerable. Don't quit. Always, Dad.

JACK (O.S.). I wish I could devote more time to reading. Sometimes, it's hard to find the time.

KATIE. I never read any books...I mean, just magazines and stuff.

(*She places the book back on the shelf.* **KATIE** *crosses to the carousel and picks it up, studying it.*)

JACK (O.S.). What about school?

KATIE. I quit after the eleventh grade, and I didn't pay much attention before that.

(**JACK** *comes out dressed casually. He immediately sees* **KATIE** *touching the carousel.*)

JACK. No, no, no!

KATIE. What?

JACK. Please don't touch it. It's very fragile.

KATIE. I won't break it!

JACK. It's already broken.

(**JACK** *takes the carousel from her and looks into her eyes. He takes a moment.*)

I'm trying to repair it.

(**JACK** *sets the carousel down.*)

Why did you quit?

KATIE. For what I do, I don't need a diploma.

(**KATIE** *pushes him into the chair and kneels down in front of him. She provocatively touches his thighs and places her hands between his legs.* **JACK** *squirms looking for a way out. He notices a crucifix on her neck and touches it.* **KATIE** *suddenly pulls back.*)

JACK. Do you always wear this?

KATIE. Yes!

JACK. (*sadly*) I did too. (*pause*) Once.

KATIE. I went into a coma when I was three. My mom put this around my neck and sat with me day and night till I woke up. She told me it saved my life and that I should never take it off. So I don't.

JACK. Tell me about her.

KATIE. I'm not talking about my mom while I'm giving you a frickin' blow job. That's sick!

(**JACK** *takes her hands and lifts her up.* **KATIE** *resists.*)

I need to get this done.

JACK. What's your hurry?

KATIE. I'm getting tired.

JACK. Then why don't you go to sleep, and I'll wake you in the morning.

KATIE. Are you crazy? I'm here to fuck!

JACK. Excuse me?

KATIE. Fuck? You've heard of it?

JACK. Yes, I've heard of –

KATIE. You pay me, I fuck you, I go home! That's how it works. That's why you picked me up.

JACK. No, it's not. (*beat*) I wanted to talk –

KATIE. Then hire a fricken therapist!

JACK. I wanted to talk..to you.

KATIE. Why?

JACK. (*beat*) You remind me of my Goddaughter.

(**KATIE** *backs up.*)

KATIE. Whoa. I'm not playing that game.

JACK. No, it's not like that. (*beat*) When I saw you in that checkout line, I felt...sorry for you.

KATIE. Don't do me any favors.

JACK. I'm not...I'm doing myself one. She ran away two years ago and died in this city. It destroyed my partner and his wife.

KATIE. That's not your fault.

JACK. I could have helped her, but they wouldn't hear of it. When I saw you standing there and you didn't have the money, it was like I was...

(**JACK** *struggles to find the word then...*)

KATIE. Just...talk?

JACK. Why not? It doesn't sound like you have anyone waiting for you at home.

KATIE. No, but I –

JACK. Then what's the problem? It's cold as hell out there. This is a nice place, don't you think?

KATIE. Yeah, it's nice. How did you know how to get all the right stuff? Stuff that matched?

JACK. I hired an interior decorator.

KATIE. That's what I want to do.

JACK. Really?

KATIE. (*offended*) I don't plan on spending the rest of my life on my knees. This is only temporary till I can save enough money.

JACK. For what?

KATIE. To get my education. I know I'll never be able to afford anything like this, so I want to be able to buy beautiful things and put them up in other people's houses.

(**KATIE** *crosses to a painting on the wall and stares at it.*)

Except this.

JACK. Doesn't speak to you?

KATIE. If it is, it's saying, "I look like shit!"

(**JACK** *laughs and takes the painting down.*)

Hey, don't do it for me.

JACK. It's okay. For the amount of money I paid, it should be talking to *everyone* in the building. Then it's settled. You can stay in the guest room.

KATIE. (*disbelief*) I'm *not* sleeping with you?

(*A moment, as* **KATIE** *looks him over. Suddenly she grabs* *her bag and crosses to the door.*)

This is too weird for me.

(**KATIE** *turns to* **JACK**.)

I have never talked to any man this fucking long in my whole life.

JACK. But...but what about the money?

KATIE. What about it?

JACK. All we did was talk.

KATIE. Then you got what you paid for, right? Don't cry, here's a hundred back...I feel generous.

(*She throws one bill on the floor and reaches for the door.*)

JACK. Please stay!

KATIE. I'm out of here.

JACK. Wait!

(**JACK** *picks up the bill from the floor and crosses to the door and puts the money in her open purse.*)

I want you to have it. I mean, if you have to go. (*beat*) Thanks for just talking to me.

(**JACK** *crosses back to the piano and starts to quietly play as* **KATIE** *partially opens the door and reconsiders.*)

KATIE. You're not going to hurt me, are you?

JACK. Never. Why would you say that?

KATIE. 'Cause I've been with some scary fuckers lately.

JACK. I'm not sure I want to ask this, but like how do you mean, scary?

(**JACK** *stops playing and crosses to* **KATIE**.)

KATIE. Oh, like a necrophiliac that has me take an ice cold bath and then lie totally still while he fucks me.

JACK. (*cautiously*) Okay –

KATIE. Or the girls' volley ball coach that insists I wear a catholic school uniform and a pony tail while he puts a ruler to my butt and bangs me at the same time –

JACK. I get the idea –

KATIE. Or my personal favorite...one of New York's finest who likes to practice his techniques of "prisoner restraints" as he ties up my little ass and wails away like I'm a –

JACK. Okay...okay! I can assure you that I would never even think to do any of the above.

KATIE. I don't know. You could be as strange. I've been here for forty minutes, and I haven't gone down on you.

JACK. Would that make you feel more secure?

KATIE. You bet it would. (*beat*) Wait a minute. Are you gay?

JACK. No, I'm not.

KATIE. Oh, I know. You're one of those weird religious fanatics.

JACK. No. I'm agnostic.

(**KATIE** *doesn't understand.*)

It means I doubt the existence of God.

KATIE. Don't say that! Don't say it around me.

JACK. Interesting, a religious hooker.

KATIE. Mary Magdalene was a big player in the bible.

JACK. If you believe it –

KATIE. Hey, stop it. I don't want to get hit by the bolt of lightning if *He* misses your ass.

JACK. I think we'll be fine.

(**JACK** *silently sits.* **KATIE** *crosses to him and sits down.*)

KATIE. This is your first time with a hooker, isn't it?

JACK. Does it show?

KATIE. You're married.

JACK. (*pause*) Divorced.

KATIE. Terrible, right?

JACK. Not the first few years. They were special.

KATIE. Kids?

JACK. I'd rather not go there now.

KATIE. A lot of you guys feel guilty. I'll get some Kleenex.

JACK. I won't cry. I come from a long line of stoic people. Caring, just not very demonstrative.

(**KATIE** *looks curiously at him.*)

They had a difficult time showing their love.

(**KATIE** *takes a moment.*)

KATIE. You were lucky. My father just *didn't* care, at least not about us, and my mother had enough to do just trying to stay alive.

JACK. I'm sorry.

KATIE. Uh...stoic?

JACK. Resolute. (*beat*) Steadfast in the face of adversity or danger.

KATIE. Uh-huh.

JACK. When did you say you quit school?

KATIE. Eleventh grade. Why?

JACK. Can I give you some advice?

KATIE. It's your money.

JACK. You say you want to advance yourself. You can start with your vocabulary. Try to use one word that isn't an obscenity every day...a different word. Incongruent. Stoic.

KATIE. Why?

JACK. People will look at you differently.

KATIE. I don't think anyone that picks me up cares about my vocabulary.

JACK. Really?

(*A moment.*)

KATIE. It's better than being ignored.

(**JACK** *sadly looks at her.*)

What?

JACK. Nothing.

KATIE. You're fucking weird.

JACK. Maybe. (*beat*) Probably. We can figure it all out tomorrow. We'll have breakfast and then I'd like to take you out.

KATIE. Where?

JACK. Everywhere and anywhere you want to go, whatever you want to do. Please your heart.

(**KATIE** *drops her head and a tear comes to her eyes.*)

KATIE. That's a lot of time. (*beat*) I'm...expensive.

JACK. I can afford it. (*beat*) I'll give you...let's see...a thousand dollars for the day.

KATIE. A thousand bucks?

(**JACK** *nods. A moment.*)

What do you get out of it?

JACK. Your company and...maybe some of my guilt appeased.

KATIE. (*beat*) Doing this with me won't bring her back.

JACK. I know that, but still, it makes me feel better. Good night, Serena. You can stay in the guest bedroom right down the hall. Lock the door...if you like.

(**KATIE** *crosses to the guest bedroom door.*)

KATIE. Hey, my name ain't Serena, it's Katie.

JACK. Thank you for that.

(**KATIE** *opens the bedroom door.* **JACK** *stops her.*)

Hey, Katie. (*beat*) I'm not divorced.

KATIE. Thank you for that.

(**JACK** *crosses to her. He places his hand on her face and leans in to kiss her on the lips but* **KATIE** *diverts the kiss to her cheek.*)

Good night, Jacko!

(**KATIE** *exits to the guest bedroom as* **JACK** *touches his fingers to his lips. He smiles.*)

Good night, Katie.

(**JACK** *crosses to the piano. He sits and plays his unfinished opus. The lights fade to black.*)

Scene III

Setting: The same as in Act I Scene I. Present time.

(*Katie's picture is returned.* **KATIE** *stands in front of the guest bedroom door.* **JULIA** *is at the piano.*)

KATIE. I was so freaked that night. I slept with one leg hanging over the bed for a quick escape.

JULIA. (*shocked*) You'll have to excuse me. I'm somewhat... *dismayed* right now. Jack...with a...prostitute. (*beat*) How did one afternoon turn into six months?

KATIE. It's crazy I know. The first day he wakes me up at eight in the morning. I didn't even know that people were alive at that hour. He takes me to breakfast and then tries to show me Manhattan in twenty-four hours.

JULIA. And the next day?

KATIE. Same stuff. Up early and out all day. Museums, art galleries, restaurants. Well Monday came, I got my money, and I was walking out the door, and then he hits me with his "business plan". He tells me that he's in Manhattan two weekends a month, and he wants me to be here for him. *Pays* me eight thousand bucks for the month...and he's only here six days.

JULIA. (*shocked*) Eight thousand –

KATIE. Dollars! I almost lost it when he dropped the cash in my hands. But there *were* conditions...as he calls them. I couldn't do anymore tricks, with anyone...he made me promise.

JULIA. That's it?

KATIE. And, I had to save any money I didn't need to live on during the week for my education.

JULIA. You must be *really* special.

KATIE. I never thought of myself like that, but he does.

JULIA. Yes. (*beat*) And he got what...for eight –

KATIE. Thousand bucks! A date when he was in town... someone to share all the things he loves with.

JULIA. I see.

KATIE. And, as he put it, "to give some meaning to his Goddaughter's death."

JULIA. His Goddaughter? Yes. Yes. That was sad. And living here...how did that come about?

KATIE. He offered, and I really didn't have a place of my own, so I figured...why not? I just couldn't have any wild parties. It's a pretty quiet building.

JULIA. And you were here for...the money?

KATIE. At first but after a really short time I realized I was *supposed* to be here.

JULIA. I'm not sure I understand.

KATIE. I didn't either...until I fell in love with him. Now everything makes sense.

JULIA. You believe in fate?

KATIE. I believe in God. I believe he steers us in directions we're supposed to go.

JULIA. That won't help you. Jack drove away from God a long time ago.

(**KATIE** *smiles and waves her finger at* **JULIA**)

KATIE. Maybe you don't know your brother as well as you think you do.

(*A moment.*)

JULIA. You've got a big job ahead of you, Katie. Jack *doesn't* change.

KATIE. He does for me.

JULIA. What makes you different? What makes a solidly established man, a good man, pick up a prostitute and play house with her?

KATIE. Because he *is* a good man. And we aren't playing.

JULIA. You don't take your charity to bed with you.

KATIE. I'm not a charity, and I told you, it didn't start like –

(**JULIA** *walks away from her.*)

JULIA. It doesn't matter how it started. It isn't right.

KATIE. You don't think I'm good enough for your brother.

JULIA. I didn't say that.

KATIE. But that's what you think.

(**KATIE** *crosses to the carousel.*)

JULIA. This is completely out of character for him. I walk in here and all of a sudden everything I knew to be true about him...isn't.

KATIE. Because he loves me?

(**KATIE** *touches the carousel.*)

JULIA. How could he love you?

(**JULIA** *crosses and guards the carousel.* **KATIE** *retreats.*)

KATIE. Why does anyone love anyone? He's attracted to me.

JULIA. Yes, okay, that's a start. But there has to be more. More than looks to base a lifetime of companionship on. What do you have in common with him?

KATIE. At first...nothing.

JULIA. And now?

KATIE. Everything.

JULIA. (*doubting*) Everything?

(**KATIE** *thinks and after a moment crosses to the piano.*)

KATIE. Beethoven cut the legs off of his piano so he could feel the vibrations on the floor.

JULIA. Your point?

(**KATIE** *crosses to the bookshelf and removes a book.*)

KATIE. William Stewart Halsted...the father of modern surgery, was a homosexual cocaine addict that experimented on his students and some of them died. It's all in here.

JULIA. What does that have to do with –

(*A moment.* **KATIE** *crosses to a painting on the wall.*)

KATIE. Some of Vincent Van Gogh's greatest works are his

Sunflower pieces. He went nuts. Cut his ear off and then gave it to a prostitute as a gift.

(**KATIE** *is very proud.*)

JULIA. I can assure you Jack is not going to cut off any part of –

KATIE. No! Don't you see…music, literature, art…everything.

JULIA. Not really.

KATIE. What else is there?

JULIA. History. (*beat*) Experiencing a similar pain. Jack lost his brother. Do you know what that does to a man?

KATIE. I don't have a brother but I –

JULIA. Can you understand what it's like to watch your child die…a little bit each day…and be unable to help her.

KATIE. You're turning this all around –

JULIA. You're just a kid! You're not ready to be with a man like Jack. There's been two lifetimes before he ever met you.

KATIE. Okay. I haven't lived his life. I haven't had his dreams, but all of that is in the past. I am his future. We will make a life together, and I'll give him everything that she wasn't able to.

JULIA. You can't.

KATIE. I will. I lived with parents who had a bad marriage. I won't make those mistakes.

JULIA. His wife had history and children with him and she couldn't keep him. What makes you think you'll be able to?

KATIE. Because I won't crawl inside myself to hide from a man who loves me.

JULIA. Is that what you think happened to them?

KATIE. She blamed him for everything but it takes two to make a baby. She knew the risks as well as he. She said yes.

JULIA. You're talking about things you couldn't possibly understand.

KATIE. I understand Jack and I know what he needs.

JULIA. Oh my God! You're proof he doesn't know what he needs.

(*A moment.*)

KATIE. I thought you were going to be my friend. I thought I finally had someone I could talk to. I guess I was wrong. (*beat*)
I think you should leave.

JULIA. You're throwing me out?

KATIE. What's the point of you staying? You don't care for –

(**JULIA** *backs off.*)

JULIA. Look, you can't expect me to accept all this immediately. I don't even know you. (*beat*) I'm confused. How did this go from a business relationship to...to...love?

(*The phone rings.* **JULIA** *starts to go for the phone than hesitates.* **KATIE** *looks at the phone but doesn't answer it.*)

Are you going to answer that?

(*Phone rings.*)

KATIE. It's Jack. I'll take it in my room...if you don't mind.

(*The phone rings again.* **KATIE** *enters the guest bedroom. As the lights go to black,* **JULIA** *exits, Katie's picture is removed, and a blank panel remains.*)

Scene IV

Setting: The same. Four months earlier.

(*The lights resume, depicting a time four months earlier. The phone keeps ringing.*)

JACK. (*calling out to* KATIE) Katie. Katie, grab that.
(*loudly*) Katie.

(JACK *enters from the master bedroom and picks up the phone.*)

(*on phone*) Yes. Susan, I'm sorry. Okay. March 15th? Perfect. Thanks. I'll be in the office Tuesday. Goodbye, Susan.

(JACK *hangs up and checks his desk calendar.*)

Katie.

KATIE (O.S.). What!

JACK. What are you doing in there?

(JACK *eyes the apartment, picks up his recorder, and dictates.*)

(*dictating*) Susan, remind me to give you the number of that maid service I used last month for the New York place. (*Beat.*) Katie!

(JACK *sits at his desk and begins to work. After a few moments,* KATIE *enters from the guest bedroom carrying a painting. She clears her throat several times to get* JACK'S *attention.*)

What are you doing?

(JACK *looks up.*)

KATIE. Happy...whatever!

JACK. You're not supposed to be spending your money on me.

KATIE. It's okay. I don't have anyone else left to spend it on.

(KATIE *turns the painting around.* JACK *steps back. The painting depicts a man and woman. This is the*

painting that appears in Act I Scene I.)
Well?

JACK. I love this. Thank you. You've got a good eye.

KATIE. You really like it?

JACK. I wouldn't have said it if I didn't mean it. (*beat*) What is it?

KATIE. I'm just not used to that.

JACK. Well *get* used to it. (*beat*) Here, help me a second.

(**JACK** *and* **KATIE** *put the painting on the wall where the first painting had been removed. They both step back and look at it.*)

KATIE. The colors...it's almost like the artist is touching the face of God.

JACK. Is that what you see?

KATIE. Don't you?

JACK. I'm agnostic, remember?

KATIE. Just because you lost your brother is no reason to give up on God.

JACK. *He* gave up on me.

KATIE. I don't think God gets involved in the small stuff.

JACK. My brother dying of Cystic Fibrosis is small to you?

KATIE. No, that's very sad but it's all in the plan, you know. We can't figure God out. You'd better put that crucifix back on before He really gets pissed at you.

JACK. I'm afraid that's never going to happen.

KATIE. It saved *my* life. You ought to –

(**KATIE** *grimaces and holds the right side of her abdomen*)

JACK. What is it?

(*After a moment,* **KATIE** *straightens up.*)

KATIE. Just a cramp. I'm fine.

JACK. Hey, I got great news for you.

KATIE. We're going to sleep in the same bed?

JACK. No...better. Your G.E.D. is scheduled for March 15.

KATIE. (*sarcastic*) Oh joy.

JACK. That's right. So you need to hit the books, and I have some work I *have* to finish.

KATIE. I'm not supposed to be studying on the weekends when you're here. That was your rule.

JACK. I know, but you're only one month away. You'll need every day and if I don't get this done, I'm going to have court sanctions.

(**JACK** *sits at his desk and works.* **KATIE** *crosses stage left and sits at the kitchen bar. She opens the shutter, leans in and grabs her Biology book.*)

(*dictating*) Susan, ask Lou where we stand with the motion for the stay against World Communications –

KATIE. What are you working on that's so important?

JACK. An alleged corporate failure to disclose a material fact.

KATIE. What?

JACK. I'm defending a corporation that failed to tell their shareholders details regarding the eventual sale of the company.

KATIE. They lied to them.

JACK. Indirectly, that's true, but they lied for a reason.

KATIE. Since when is it okay to lie for any reason?

JACK. It depends on the situation. I mean...sometimes... even in relationships, we have to lie to one another, don't we?

KATIE. What kind of relationship is that?

JACK. It can be a good one.

KATIE. Then why are they lying to each other?

(*A moment as* **JACK** *thinks.* **KATIE** *crosses to his desk.*)

That's one thing I don't put up with. A guy lies to me, it's over.

(*She puts her arms around him and starts to kiss him. He gently pulls away. He turns on the recorder.*)

JACK. You'd better get back to work.

(*A rejected* **KATIE** *crosses back to the kitchen bar stool. On the way she stops to touch the carousel.* **JACK** *admonishes her with a stare causing her to stop. She sits on the bar stool rubs the sweat off her forehead.*)

(*dictating*) Susan, on page 15, Section 2.1 of Veloz versus Taylor, we need to –

KATIE. Fucking Biology! Dominant and recessive traits. Stupid little jig saw puzzle and percentages.

(**JACK** *is annoyed and stops dictating.*)

JACK. It's pretty important stuff.

KATIE. For who?

JACK. Whom. (*beat*) Anyone who carries a bad trait.

KATIE. So what? According to this, they're not the ones that are sick.

(**JACK** *throws his pencil down.*)

JACK. I am never going to finish this.

(**JACK** *rises and picks up a few chess pieces from the playing board behind the couch. He sits on the couch and places the pieces on the coffee table as* **KATIE** *crosses to him with her book.*)

(*beat*) Okay, let me see if this helps. Imagine this king here is my father, and he carries the trait for Cystic Fibrosis. And this queen over here is my mother, and she also carries the trait for Cystic Fibrosis. Alone, they're very healthy. But when they meet, fall in love, and have children – and we'll let these pawns be the kids – there are three possibilities. They can be normal; they can be a carrier; or twenty-five percent of the time, they will actually have the horrible disease and die. I was lucky; my brother Danny…wasn't. My wife was lucky; her twin sister Laura wasn't.

(**JACK** *rises and hands* **KATIE** *a pawn.*)

You see, a little bit more than a "stupid" puzzle.

(**JACK** *crosses back to his desk and notices his coffee mug is empty.* **KATIE** *is notably uncomfortable and rubs her right side.*)

I need another cup. You want anything?

(**KATIE** *shakes her head no.* **JACK** *crosses to the kitchen.* **KATIE** *rises and has a severe cramp which bends her over. After a moment, she straightens up and crosses to Jack's desk. She picks up his wallet and looks at a picture of Jack's deceased daughter, Sarah.*)

KATIE. So *that's* why you married her.

JACK (O.S.). What are you talking about?

KATIE. You have *this* disease in common. Your brother and her twin sister Laura. Is that why you guys hooked up?

(**JACK** *reenters.* **KATIE** *puts down the wallet.*)

JACK. That's how we met. At a picnic at Central Park. A support group for Cystic Fibrosis. (*beat*) Our lives changed on that carousel.

(*A moment.*)

KATIE. You got a marriage grounded on two dead people. No wonder you picked me up.

JACK. Back to work wise ass.

(**KATIE** *reluctantly crosses to her books and quickly becomes irritated.*)

KATIE. (*sarcastically*) Language!

JACK. (*with a clenched jaw*) Please let me get through this.

(**KATIE** *rubs her right lower side and crosses to the couch and sits.*)

Susan, again page 14, Section 2, paragraph –

KATIE. It's page 15!

JACK. Yes, page 15, Section 2 –

KATIE. Damn it! I'm feeling all...all

(**KATIE** *searches for the word.*)

...closed in here.

(**JACK** *continues to write at his desk and doesn't look up.*)

JACK. Here's an opportunity. Give me another?

KATIE. God dammit!

(**JACK** *turns on the recorder.*)

JACK. Check your book!
(*dictating*) The execution and delivery of this agreement by each of the parties –

(**KATIE** *looks through her notebook.*)

KATIE. Claustrophobic?

(**KATIE** *is sweating now and removes her sweater tossing it behind the couch.*)

JACK. That's right. It's simple. You'll get it.

KATIE. I don't think I want to get it.

JACK. It's important that you do.

KATIE. For who?

JACK. Whom!

KATIE. Shit! I'm wasting my time. Can you help me?

JACK. I'll get you another tutor.

KATIE. I don't want another tutor. You do it!

JACK. I don't know everything. I'll *call* a tutor –

KATIE. (*nasty*) Don't break your finger –

JACK. (*irritated*) Katie –

KATIE. Take me out!

JACK. Will you just grow up and do it!

KATIE. All right. All right.

(**KATIE** *sits on the stool and picks up the books. She is more uncomfortable and irritated.* **JACK** *rubs his eyes, looks over the apartment and then picks up the recorder.*)

JACK. (*dictating*) Susan, it's called Maid For You in New York. This place really needs it.

(*A moment.*)

(*feeling guilty*) Okay. How about no work tomorrow? For either of us. We can go out.

KATIE. Where?

JACK. You name it?

KATIE. There's a free concert tomorrow night.

(**KATIE** *crosses to* **JACK**.)

JACK. We don't have to go to a free concert.

KATIE. Just because it's free doesn't mean it's shit.

JACK. I didn't say it was. I'm just –

KATIE. A fucking snob.

(**KATIE** *crosses into the guest bedroom.*)

JACK. That's totally unfair.

KATIE (O.S.). Just admit it…you're a fucking snob.

JACK. I'm only giving you the benefit of my experience. Why waste your time learning what I already know?

KATIE (O.S.). Because experiencing it is what's fun. Making the mistakes, that's what's interesting. (*beat*) I bet you even did everything your parents wanted you to.

(**JACK** *thinks.*)

JACK. Yes. (*beat*) Mostly.

(**KATIE** *enters with a jacket*)

KATIE. I'm not surprised. Frickin' boring. Oh, you are so…

(*She looks into her notebook.*)

Repugnant!

(**KATIE** *throws the book into the guest room hallway and crosses to the door.*)

JACK. Where are you going?

KATIE. Out. Out with the poor people.

JACK. That wasn't the plan.

KATIE. I'm skipping the plan. Tell you the truth, I feel like giving *someone* a blow job.

(**KATIE** *opens the door.*)

JACK. Katie! I know what you –

KATIE. You don't know me. You don't know the first thing about me.

JACK. I'm trying to –

KATIE. You write a check. You take out a credit card. Make a call. That's easy for you. Try doing something that really requires putting yourself out there.

JACK. I'm doing the best I can.

KATIE. And I'm sick of it. You're suffocating me. You can't keep me here by buying me things and shoving Social Studies down my throat.

JACK. It was part of your plan. I thought you wanted to pass the G.E.D.

KATIE. I thought I did, too. I can't do this anymore.

JACK. There are times when you have to be responsible.

KATIE. And where's it gotten you? You did it all right. Followed all the rules. Big success. Now look at you. You're spending your weekends with a teenage hooker.

JACK. I want you to succeed. I want you to be able to do wonderful things with your life. To be independent –

KATIE. What the hell does it matter to you?

(**JACK** *is being backed into a corner.*)

JACK. I told you. My Godchild –

KATIE. Bullshit! That's not good enough. Tell me!

(**KATIE** *grimaces in pain as she rubs her side.*)

JACK. Because. Because I...it just does.

KATIE. Why? (*beat*) Why do you care so frickin' much?

(*They stare uncomfortably at each other.* **JACK** *starts to speak and then backs down.*)

I'm out of here. I'm sure you can find yourself someone else to rescue!

(**KATIE** *opens the door to leave and bends over with pain.*)

JACK. Katie, what is it.

KATIE. Oh my God. This hurts.

(**JACK** *crosses to her.*)

Leave me alone.

(*She falls to her knees.* **JACK** *crosses to her.*)

JACK. Katie, you're burning up. Where does it hurt you?

KATIE. Right here.

(*She points to her lower right side. He pushes on it.*)

Don't push! God, Mr. Gentle.

JACK. I'm sorry. I'm sorry. I think that's your appendix. I've got to get you to the hospital.

KATIE. I can't even walk!

(**JACK** *carries her to the couch.*)

JACK. I'm calling 911. We need an ambulance.

(**JACK** *crosses to the phone. He dials.*)

KATIE. I'll be all right. I don't want to go to the hospital.

JACK. (*on phone*) My emergency? I think it's acute appendicitis. Katie McDaniels. No, I'm *not* Katie. I'm Jack. Jack Davis. I'm at 125 East 83rd Street. Between Lexington and Park. Apartment 44 G. Okay. Okay. Hurry.

(**JACK** *hangs up the phone and quickly crosses to* **KATIE** *at the couch.*)

They'll be here soon. I'm only five blocks away from Lenox Hill.

KATIE. I feel like shit.

(**JACK** *picks her up in his arms and puts her on his lap.*)

JACK. I'm sorry for making such a big deal about the stupid exam.

KATIE. No, you were right. (*beat*) I have to tell you something.

(*She moans in pain.*)

JACK. Don't talk. It can wait.

KATIE. I'm scared.

JACK. It's not a big deal. It's a real small cut. You'll be out in no time. I think they do them through a –

KATIE. Stop talking. It's not my appendix!

JACK. You don't know that.

KATIE. Yes. I do.

JACK. How can you be sure?

KATIE. Because I had it out four years ago. (*beat*) Oh my God, I can't tell you this. It's going to ruin everything.

JACK. What is it?

KATIE. I think I...I think I may be...pregnant.

JACK. Pregnant?

KATIE. Jack, I'm so sorry. It was one of my regulars. He called. I told him where I was.

(*Jack rises, shifts her off his lap and crosses away from her.*)

JACK. You let him in here?

KATIE. It was before I really knew you. It was before I –

JACK. You turned a trick in my home?

KATIE. I didn't plan it. He's a friend. We got carried away. He told me that I would be crazy to give up my regulars. He kept talking and the more he talked the more unsure I felt.

JACK. (*sarcastically*) Great advice. Great friend.

KATIE. Who *are* you, Jack? I had no idea. It was in the first week. How was I to know you were serious? What if it didn't last? I didn't know you then.

JACK. We had a deal.

KATIE. Please Jack. I felt horrible afterward. I didn't even take his money.

JACK. I trusted you –

KATIE. And you can keep trusting me.

JACK. How? How can I do that?

KATIE. Because I'm begging you to. Because I made a mistake –

JACK. That *I'll* have to live with.

KATIE. (*angrily*) I'm not asking you to. It's my problem.

(*A moment.*)

JACK. No Katie. (*beat*) It's our problem.
 You certainly know how to complicate a relationship.

KATIE. I swear to you, Jack. There's been no one since and it won't ever happen again. I've been making deals with God all –

(**KATIE** *starts to cry.*)

JACK. You don't have to make any deals. Try to stay still, the ambulance will be here any minute.

KATIE. Will you hold me?

(**JACK** *picks her up and holds her in his arms. He sits on the couch with her.*)

JACK. What happened to your moral stand on lying?

KATIE. It's not technically a lie. Is it? I mean, you never *really* asked me.

JACK. You might want to consider politics as a career.

(**KATIE** *tries to get comfortable. He gently touches her hair. After a few moments.*)

KATIE. Who is Sarah?

(**JACK** *is taken off guard. He tenses up and is uncomfortable.*)

In your wallet. There's a picture. It says, "Sarah, age thirteen. Is she your daughter?

JACK. (*beat*) She was. We lost her two years ago.

KATIE. She's so pretty. What was she like?

JACK. We don't have to talk about this now. I'll tell you about it –

KATIE. I want to.

(*A moment*)

JACK. The day she died she was more worried about me.

KATIE. You miss her?

(**KATIE** *grimaces in pain and embraces* **JACK** *very tightly.*)

JACK. Okay, enough talk.

(*The door buzzer rings.*)

Here we go. I'll bring them up.

(**JACK** *lifts* **KATIE** *and puts her on the couch. He rises and crosses to the door.*)

KATIE. Jack, I'm sorry. (*beat*) You'll stay with me?
JACK. Always.

(**JACK** *opens the door and quickly exits closing the door behind him. The lights go to black.*)

Scene V

Setting: The same. Present time.

(*As the lights resume,* **KATIE** *is on the couch as* **JULIA** *stands over her.*)

JULIA. So where is the baby?

KATIE. No baby. It was just a ruptured cyst.

JULIA. You're lucky. A child would have complicated "the business plan".

KATIE. I don't think it would have mattered to Jack.

JULIA. You really think he would have taken care of a child that wasn't his?

KATIE. Yes...as long as I was with him. As long as *I* put the child first...like he did with Sarah.

JULIA. What's that supposed to mean?

KATIE. I don't think Jack was happy that his wife was so involved with her job, especially when Sarah was sick.

JULIA. She worked at four a.m. Sarah was still asleep by the time she got home.

KATIE. Still...my mother was always with me when I was little.

JULIA. She was *there* Katie!

KATIE. Yeah, she was there. Making him feel guilty every day for even wanting a child.

(**JULIA'S** *anger grows.*)

JULIA. It's not true!

KATIE. That's what I heard.

JULIA. She never left her alone. He was the one who wasn't there!

KATIE. I'm sure that's her side of the story.

JULIA. It's not a story. It's the truth.

KATIE. How would *you* know that?

(*A moment as* **JULIA** *boils.*)

JULIA. That's it! Just...get...out!

KATIE. Excuse me?

JULIA. I'm afraid there is no excuse for you.

KATIE. What did I do?

JULIA. *You* exist.

KATIE. *I* live here!

JULIA. *I* want you out. Now! I'm not going to listen to this anymore.

KATIE. You're his sister. I belong here more than you do. You got no right throwing me out.

JULIA. His sister wouldn't, but his *wife* would! Now, take your teenage self, your cheap underwear, and your inappropriate use of a thesaurus and leave...now!

KATIE. (*disbelief*) You're his wife?

JULIA. Let's see if you can read.

(**JULIA** *pulls her car registration from her pocketbook.*)

I realize the "big" words may confuse you, but this is my car registration. Owner: Julia and Jack Davis.

(**KATIE** *reads the card.*)

KATIE. He hasn't been with his wife in years.

JULIA. What are you talking about? He lives at our home.

KATIE. He wouldn't lie to me.

JULIA. He's lied to both of us. God, what an idiot I've been. I want you out of here.

(**KATIE** *presses her back up against the wall and crosses her arms.*)

KATIE. I'm waiting for Jack.

JULIA. No you're not. Get out!

KATIE. Fuck you.

JULIA. What, no big words? A simple...fuck you?

KATIE. Well, I'm sorry I'm not like your frickin' Harvard educated daughter.

JULIA. It's Stanford and that's not the only way you're not like her. She doesn't sleep around with men more than twice her age. She doesn't destroy families. Now, I'm going to call the doorman and have you thrown out.

(**JULIA** *crosses to the intercom as* **KATIE** *cuts her off.*)

KATIE. If you think I'm going to give up that easily, you don't know who you're dealing with, bitch! This is the best thing that ever happened to me.

JULIA. I'm sure.

KATIE. It's different with him.

JULIA. You're a prostitute.

KATIE. My mom needed help. I –

JULIA. How dare you! You think you can just come in here and stake claim to his property because he paid you to have sex with him?

KATIE. At least with me, he got something out of it.

JULIA. He's gotten plenty out of it. Twenty years of love and children.

KATIE. Wait a minute. (*beat*) Children? Stanford? Jack told me. Only one child...and she's *dead*.

(*A moment as the breath is knocked out of* **JULIA**.)

JULIA. Sarah is gone, but Laura is doing just fine. I can't believe I'm explaining this to you.

(**JULIA** *opens her pocketbook and shows her a picture.*)

This is Laura at our home in Connecticut.

(**KATIE** *looks at the picture and sits down, defeated.*)

KATIE. Jack wouldn't do this.

JULIA. Apparently he's capable of more than either of us knew.

KATIE. We talked about everything. Why wouldn't he have told me about Laura?

JULIA. I guess for the same reasons that he told you about a Goddaughter that *doesn't* exist!

KATIE. Doesn't exist. I –

(**JULIA** *smiles and waves her finger at* **KATIE** *imitating her from the previous scene.*)

JULIA. Maybe you don't know him as well as you think you do. Go home, little girl. Fantasy's over.

(**KATIE** *starts to cry.*)

Save your tears for Jack. You can't stay here.

(**JULIA** *reaches for the intercom phone as* **KATIE** *grabs it and holds it close to her chest.*)

(*sarcastically*) Very mature.

KATIE. I'm waiting here for Jack. If he wants me to leave he's going to have to tell me that to my face. I need to hear it from him.

JULIA. I'm afraid that's not going to happen.

KATIE. Yes it will. You don't know him the way I do. He'll come –

JULIA. No...he won't.

KATIE. We'll see.

(**KATIE** *sits. They face off in a moment of silence.*)

I'm telling you now, I don't plan on sharing him.

(*A moment.* **JULIA** *rises and crosses to look out the window.* **JULIA** *struggles, then.*)

JULIA. Jack's dead.

KATIE. (*doubting*) Dead? Jack is dead?

(**JULIA** *nods and turns from her.*)

You must really think I'm stupid. You're not going to get rid of me that easily.

JULIA. It's the truth.

KATIE. I don't believe you and you're cruel for saying it.

JULIA. Last week. He had a ruptured aneurysm.

KATIE. Now I know you're lying. He's in great shape. I'm half his age, and I couldn't keep up with him.

JULIA. It has nothing to do with that!

(**KATIE** *takes out her cell phone.*)

KATIE. I'll call him myself.

(**KATIE** *dials. After a moment, a cell phone rings in Julia's handbag.* **KATIE** *turns white as a ghost as she stares at the handbag.* **JULIA** *pulls a newspaper clipping from her pocketbook and hands it to* **KATIE**.)

JULIA. Here.

KATIE. What is it?

JULIA. Wednesday's *Hartford Courant.* (*beat*) It's Jack's obituary.

(**KATIE** *reads the papers. The lights go to black.*)

END OF ACT I

ACT II

Scene I

Setting: The Apartment. Present time. The set is the same.

(**JULIA** *and* **KATIE** *are frozen in the same position they were at the end of Act I Scene V.*)

KATIE. Oh my God! No. Jack. No!

(**KATIE** *cries.*)

This is not happening. Not to me. Not today. Tell me you're making this up?

JULIA. You need to leave now!

KATIE. I don't want to go. This is our place. This is where he's happy.

JULIA. You knew he was a married man. You've *ruined* what we had.

KATIE. It was ruined long before I got here.

JULIA. This is *my* place now. Get out!

KATIE. (*praying*) Oh, Jesus. Please, I'm begging you.

(**KATIE** *crosses to the window and looks out.*)

I swear. I swear to you, I'll never turn another trick. I'll starve to death first. Just don't let this be true.

JULIA. You're too late.

(**KATIE** *numb, takes a moment, turns and sits on the couch.*)

KATIE. He told me the last six months he spent with *me* were the best of his life.

JULIA. The best years of his life weren't about *either* of us. It was when he held his little girl. When he dreamed about her future.

KATIE. I thought I was his future. (*beat*) I wanted to give him everything.

JULIA. (*disgusted*) What *didn't* you give him?

KATIE. (*pause*) Me.

JULIA. *You?* (*beat*) You spent every other weekend here together for six months. What did you do...play chess?

KATIE. I told you...it was a business deal to him.

JULIA. I know Jack and *I* don't believe you.

KATIE. He wanted to wait.

JULIA. For what?

> (**KATIE** *shrugs her shoulders.*)

Oh come on. Business? Who are you buying the sexy underwear for?

KATIE. Wishful thinking.

JULIA. I'm sure.

KATIE. (*angrily*) I told you, we never –

JULIA. My husband was here for six months with a prostitute and you two never...Never, at all?

> (**KATIE** *shakes her head.*)

KATIE. I'd love to tell *you* we did, but no, *never at all!*

> (**JULIA** *pauses for a moment and takes it all in.*)

JULIA. He secretly buys this apartment. He packs it with *all* of his fantasies. The piano he never mastered, the books he never read, and I suppose...you.

KATIE. I guess I wasn't his fantasy girl. I'm no one's fantasy girl.

> (*There is an uncomfortable silence.* **KATIE** *cries.* **JULIA** *softens.*)

What am I going to do?

JULIA. You should go back home.

KATIE. I can't and I won't break my promise to Jack.

JULIA. What promise?

KATIE. He was paying me a lot of money not to be with anyone else.

JULIA. No one is going to pay you anymore.

KATIE. I know that. But all the same, I can't. (*beat*) God, why would he have me take classes, study, if he wasn't going to be here to help me? I feel so stupid.

(**KATIE** *sits.*)

JULIA. He wasn't planning to die.

(**JULIA** *takes a moment and needs to be absolutely certain.*)

All right. (*beat*) If there was no sex...right?

KATIE. There was *no* sex. (*beat*) Right!

(**JULIA** *struggles to understand.*)

JULIA. What did you two do weekend after weekend?

KATIE. Experienced...everything. Went everywhere. He *hated* my clothes. He took me to Saks, Lord and Taylor, Neiman Marcus and bought me all this grown up, expensive stuff.

JULIA. You make it sound like it was a bad thing.

KATIE. Some of it was kind of old for me. Not what I like to wear. He was a bit of a fuddy duddy sometimes.

JULIA. Jack was always fifty. (*beat*) Where else did you go?

KATIE. Chuck E. Cheese.

(**JULIA** *looks at her inquisitively.*)

That's where we went on Saturdays. At first I thought he was like one of those raincoat wearing Pee Wee Herman freaks but he tells me it's 'cause he loves the pizza.

JULIA. He didn't love pizza.

KATIE. Well he loved it there. One time when I came back from the bathroom, he's gone. This little kid comes up to me and says that the man I was with gave him ten tokens to tell me to take off my shoes and go into the balls with him.

(**JULIA'S** *confused*)

You know, those little blue and red plastic balls in that big caged area.

JULIA. Okay.

KATIE. So I get in there, and all of a sudden I feel something grabbing my ankle, and Christ if it isn't Jack, who's buried himself under the balls, pulling me under. We spend the whole afternoon playing every game, pinball, basketball, air hockey. Did he do crazy stuff like that with you?

JULIA. Before Sarah was born he could make cleaning a horse stall exciting. At four a.m., he would bring his keyboard into the bedroom and play that never-ending opus! Can you imagine waking up to that every morning at four?

KATIE. I would have killed him.

JULIA. In a strange way, it really turned me on. It was the quintessential Jack being romantic.

KATIE. Why so early?

JULIA. I did the news at six a.m. and since he never slept, he got me up. (*beat*) But the best thing about him was how he talked to me...

KATIE. Tell me!

JULIA. He would always look me straight in the eyes and never veered even if we were in a crowded room. It was like I was the only one who was there. Sometimes it was unnerving but most of the time exciting to have a man that you love show you so much attention.

KATIE. I know.

(**KATIE** *begins to cry, turns and enters her room.* **JULIA** *is unaware that she has left the room.*)

JULIA. One year he insisted we take ballroom dance lessons. He was really bad at it. But he wouldn't quit. He said it didn't matter how well we floated across the room; he just loved holding me.

(**JULIA** *turns and notices* **KATIE** *is gone. As the lights fade to black, ballet music is heard.*)

Scene II

Setting: The same. Two weeks earlier, Sunday evening.

(*As the light change is completed,* **KATIE** *enters the room dressed in a dance leotard and sits on the floor and stretches.*)

KATIE. (*yelling to* **JACK**) Are you coming out?

JACK (O.S.). In a minute.

KATIE. You need to be out here before September 28th.

JACK (O.S.). Why September 28th?

KATIE. That's my twentieth birthday, and I don't want to spend it waiting for your tired ass.

JACK (O.S.). (*harshly*) Katie!

KATIE. Buttocks! Okay, buttocks. (*beat*) Jesus, he doesn't miss a thing!

(**JACK** *enters leaping across the room. He is dressed in a leotard with a black cape, cardboard helmet visor, and pieces of moldering armor. He wears a fake goatee and carries a sword. He lands in front of* **KATIE** *and swoops her up into his arms. He speaks with a suave romantic voice.*)

JACK. (*Quixote voice*) I'm here...your Don Quixote!

KATIE. Who?

JACK. (*Quixote voice*) Don Quixote...an eccentric nobleman who will fight anyone and anything in the name of love.

KATIE. And who am I?

JACK. (*Quixote voice*) Why...Dulcinea, of course.

(**JACK** *lovingly dips her.*)

KATIE. (*smiling*) I like that name.

JACK. (*Quixote voice*) Then come here, my little princess, and let me sweep you off your precious little feet and steal you away from the drudgery of your past life.

(**JACK** *takes her in his arms and playfully swings her around. He suddenly is pulled back into reality.*)

Am I hurting you?

KATIE. I'm fine.

(*He picks her up and prances around the room.*)

You're crazy.

JACK. (*in his Quixote voice*) I am the only sane man in an insane society!

(**JACK** *gently dips her back.*)

Not too shoddy for only two classes.

(**KATIE** *pulls off his goatee.*)

KATIE. You're not taking this serious.

JACK. (*indignant*) I'll have you know this costume is appropriate for the time and setting of the ballet. To do the great ballet, one must look the part.

KATIE. Let me fix it. Where in God's name did you get this?

(**KATIE** *removes his helmet.*)

JACK. What are you doing? (*beat*) My secretary...for last year's office Halloween party.

KATIE. You let your secretary pick out your clothes?

(**KATIE** *removes his cape.*)

JACK. Hey, that's my cape. (*beat*) Susan picks out everything, I'm embarrassed to admit. But she said the costume embodied the substance of my being and my place with the firm.

KATIE. A knight?

JACK. A champion of the poor, the disgruntled. Roaming the country to right the wrongs of society. (*beat*) In other words, I have the highest rate of pro bono work of any lawyer in the firm.

(**KATIE** *removes his armor leaving him in just the leotard.*)

What are you doing?

KATIE. Now we're ready to seriously practice.

(**JACK** *stands uncomfortably as if he's been stripped naked. He shyly covers his private parts.*)

JACK. Now, I feel like an idiot, and I'm going back to the castle.

(**JACK** *gathers his costume and crosses to the bedroom.*)

KATIE. Jack, come on. You promised.

(**JACK** *exits.* **KATIE**, *frustrated, rises and crosses to the desk. She sees his wallet. She picks it up.*)

Why don't you like to talk about her?

JACK (O.S.). Who?

KATIE. Sarah.

(**JACK** *doesn't respond.*)

Jack. Jack, did you hear me?

JACK (O.S.). I heard you.

(**JACK** *enters the room still dressed in the leotard but now wearing a robe.*)

It's...it's intensely personal.

(**JACK** *takes the wallet.*)

KATIE. (*sarcastic*) Yeah, right. Why would you want to discuss anything with me that was personal? I mean, I'm just an employee.

JACK. Stop it. You know you mean more to me –

KATIE. No, I understand. I'm good enough to have you dress me up like a Barbie doll and go to museums, parks –

JACK. We talk – don't we?

KATIE. Yes, about my exams, my dance classes, what I want to buy. What I want to do with my life – but what about you?

(*A moment.*)

JACK. What do you want to know?

KATIE. Tell me about Sarah. What was she like? What was she into?

JACK. She was into staying alive. She struggled every day to do as much as "normal" kids her age did. When she wasn't suffering with one infection after the other, she was spending her time in the bathroom passing every bit of food she ate...undigested. We couldn't keep weight on her no matter what we did. We spent a good part of every night keeping her nose and mouth clear so she could breathe and enjoy some of the regular things, watching TV and playing with dolls. Going out, vacations, that wasn't an option. We talked about a future I knew she would never have.

KATIE. Is that what you're running away from?

JACK. I'm not running away from anything.

KATIE. This place, Jack. You're a successful lawyer with a beautiful home in Connecticut. (*beat*) You're married. What are you doing here?

JACK. I'm working. It's more convenient for me to –

KATIE. I'm talking about us.

JACK. Us is what I'm running to. When Sarah died, our marriage went into a tailspin.

KATIE. Did you love her?

JACK. Yes, I loved her. There was a time I thought that I had met the woman I would grow old and die with.

KATIE. (*cautiously*) And now?

JACK. Now? (*beat*) I don't know anymore.

KATIE. Why don't you just divorce her and get it over with?

JACK. My father could answer that. He'd say, "son, you don't fold your cards just because you're not holding four aces."

KATIE. You see what happens when you don't believe in God? He takes your kid away and messes up your marriage.

JACK. There were problems long before we lost our daughter, Sarah.

KATIE. What do you mean?

JACK. When my wife was fifteen, her twin sister Laura was dying of Cystic Fibrosis. She cradled Laura in her arms and read to her as she slowly slipped away, taking almost every bit of emotion my wife possessed.

She sobbed for weeks, but when Sarah died, I don't remember her crying. It was like the final straw.

(*A moment for* **KATIE**.)

KATIE. If you knew you both were carriers, then why would–

JACK. It was only a twenty-five percent chance we'd have an affected child.

KATIE. Why risk it?

JACK. *I* wanted a child. I needed a child.

KATIE. What about your wife?

JACK. I talked her into it. She did it because she loved me.

KATIE. You were selfish.

JACK. Thanks, that sensitivity I can get at home.

(*A moment as* **KATIE** *pulls it all together.*)

KATIE. That's it, isn't it?

JACK. What?

KATIE. It took me six months to figure it out. This has nothing to do with your Goddaughter, does it? This is you trying to make me into what you think Sarah would have grown into. The clothes, the culture, the education –

JACK. Listen to me. (*pause*) Okay, I concede it. I enjoy doing all the things with you I might have done with her, but come on, it's *way* different with you.

KATIE. I'm finding that hard to believe.

JACK. Believe it! You and I have *nothing* to do with Sarah. But you're right. Having her was selfish and Sarah paid for it. Maybe we should have adopted. My brother and I were adopted by the same parents and they were wonderful folks. It would have spared all of us the pain.

KATIE. Adoption? There's no guarantee that you get a normal kid. I can tell you –

(*The phone rings.*)

Don't answer it!

(**KATIE** *runs to the desk and grabs the phone. They fight* *over the phone as* **JACK** *attempts to wrestle it from her.*)

JACK. That could be an important phone call –

KATIE. I don't care. This is important, too –

JACK. Give me that phone, Katie. Katie...Katie –

(**KATIE** *shuts the phone off and jams it under the couch pillows.* **JACK** *is angry.*)

I ought to paddle you –

KATIE. (*sexy*) Oh yeah, punish me big guy –

JACK. Stop it. You'd enjoy it too much.

KATIE. Such a tough lawyer in your little tutu.

(*She pulls open the robe exposing his manhood.*)

JACK. Don't you dare laugh.

KATIE. I'm not. (*beat*) You look...good.

JACK. Bullshit.

KATIE. No. You're in great shape for a man your...age.

JACK. I could stand to lose a little weight. (*beat*) If my partners could see me, they –

KATIE. Would respect the lengths you would go to please your... paramour.

JACK. Hey, you remembered. Now isn't that a nicer term?

KATIE. Nicer than, "your slut!" Yeah, it is. Okay, help me.

JACK. Do we really have to do this?

KATIE. All this was your idea. You insisted I take these stupid lessons.

(**KATIE** *turns on the ballet music.*)

JACK. Yes, *you* take the lessons.

KATIE. Hey, compromise, remember?

JACK. What do you want me to do?

KATIE. Okay, when the song builds here, you lift me.

JACK. You're kidding?

KATIE. No.

(**KATIE** *steps up on the ottoman in front of the chair and places her hands on* **JACK'S** *shoulders.*)

JACK. I've got a bad back.

KATIE. Liar. You didn't have any trouble ice skating, bowling, or sitting there for three hours in that hard bleacher seat watching the Yankees –

JACK. I'm not a dancer.

KATIE. I'm the prima ballerina, you're the lifter. Okay, here it comes. Now, now, lift me by the waist.

(**JACK** *lifts her into the air.* **KATIE** *is enjoying every second of the closeness.*)

That's it. Now slide me down real gently, slowly. That's right, hold me close...okay...good.

(**JACK** *complies. They become locked in each other's arms as* **KATIE** *presses her body against him. She leans in to kiss him. A moment, as* **JACK** *feels very uncomfortable and releases her.*)

JACK. I've got to change. We have dinner in two hours and then the ballet.

(**JACK** *exits to the bedroom.* **KATIE** *turns off the music and flops on the couch.*)

(**O.S.**) Are you changing?

KATIE. (*annoyed and not moving*) Yes.

JACK (O.S.). Hey, I have an idea.

KATIE. (*sarcastic*) I can't wait.

JACK (O.S.). What do you say we hop up to Bridgeport on Sunday?

KATIE. For what?

JACK (O.S.). I'd like to see the house you grew up in.

(*A moment.*)

KATIE. You can't.

JACK (O.S.). Why?

KATIE. (*sadly*) (*beat*) It was torn down.

(**JACK** *enters the room dressed.*)

JACK. Katie, I'm sorry. I know how important the house you grew up in can be.

KATIE. After my mom left there was nothing there for me anyway.

(*A moment*)

JACK. Where is she now?

KATIE. Well, *you* would say nowhere.

JACK. That's my belief, it doesn't mean that you –

KATIE. It's okay. I know she's better off.

JACK. I still can't conceive how you came to be here.

KATIE. I couldn't begin to make a man like you understand what it takes for a girl to make this choice. I'm not proud of what I did but I sent every dime to Mom that I didn't need to survive. Then, I buried her with the rest.

JACK. I don't know what to say.

KATIE. There's nothing to say. I'm done with all that.

(**KATIE** *crosses to* **JACK** *and puts her arms around him. She starts to kiss him.* **JACK** *gently backs off.*)

JACK. You'd better change.

(**JACK** *walks away.*)

KATIE. Why? Why back away?

JACK. I don't want us to be late.

KATIE. Jack, please. (*beat*) Stop.

(**KATIE** *crosses and tries to encourage him. She takes his hand and gently draws it towards her breast. He nervously backs up.*)

Make me happy. (*beat*) Make us both happy.

JACK. I don't think so.

KATIE. I do.

JACK. This was business…remember?

KATIE. It's *way* different, remember? Can you deny it's not more now?

JACK. I'm not denying anything…it's just not the right time.

KATIE. Well, what time does it have to be?

JACK. I don't know, but it's definitely not now.

KATIE. What is it? Is it me? I don't bite, you know. I'm clean. I haven't been with anyone since that first week I met you –

JACK. I know that.

KATIE. Do you? We've been together forty days in the last six months. Every museum and cultural event in this city. Eaten at almost every restaurant. Parks, concerts. You've spent, what, I don't know, maybe ten thousand dollars on clothes and jewelry for me. You've paid for tutors, bought my books to get a G.E.D...for what? Am I an experiment? A tax deduction? What happens when you get tired of me? Do I get to keep the clothes? I *don't* understand what you're doing with me.

JACK. I care about you.

KATIE. Oh that's good. (*pause*) 'Cause I...love you.

(**JACK** *is embarrassed.*)

I've never been treated like this by –

JACK. And you should never accept anything less. Remember that. From any man.

KATIE. That's fine but I don't want *any* man; I want you. And I want more.

(**JACK** *steps back and tries to lighten her up.*)

JACK. "What satisfaction canst thou have to-night?"

(**KATIE** *is frustrated.* **JACK** *waves his finger at her.*)

We read it, and we saw it.

KATIE. I hate Billy fucking Shakespeare.

JACK. You don't remember.

(**KATIE** *will not be beat.*)

KATIE. "The exchange of thy love's faithful vow for mine."

JACK. "I gave thee mine before thou did request it. And yet I would it were to give again."

(**KATIE** *walks away from him.*)

What's wrong?

KATIE. The scene is with *Romeo and Juliet*. Not Juliet and frickin' Friar Lawrence! Most couples after this amount of time take that word "love" and try it out. Touch, kiss, hold –

JACK. I hold you.

KATIE. In a weird way.

JACK. I don't want to rush it.

KATIE. It's been six months, and you haven't even kissed me.

JACK. (*imitating Clark Gable*) "You need kissing badly, that's what's wrong with you. You should be kissed and often and by someone who knows how."

KATIE. Is that supposed to be funny?

JACK. It's supposed to be Clark Gable. *Gone with the Wind.* Margaret –

KATIE. Whatever.

JACK. I *have* kissed you.

KATIE. On the cheek, on the forehead. Christ, you lock your door at night.

JACK. How do you know that?

KATIE. 'Cause I've tried to get in. God, at this rate, you'll be getting social security, and I'll have cobwebs between my legs. Now damn it, kiss me.

(*She quickly turns to him and kisses him on the lips. He quickly breaks it off.*)

JACK. No! Katie, no!

KATIE. You hate me!

JACK. I don't.

KATIE. Oh my God. I know what I've done isn't...

(*She struggles to find the word.*)

Isn't...acceptable to a man like you but that part of my life is over, and I want to make love to you. I want to feel like a real person! You won't even give me that.

(**KATIE** *runs into the guest bedroom.*)

JACK. Katie, wait. It's not you. It's me.

(**KATIE** *appears in the doorway.*)

KATIE. What is it?

JACK. Okay, here goes. (*beat*) It's all very technical and –

KATIE. (*impatiently*) Get on with it!

JACK. The local nerves are not allowing the muscles of the corpora cavernosa to relax, which would allow blood to flow in and fill the spaces. The lack of blood fails to create the pressure in the corpora cavernosa making expansion...impossible.

KATIE. (*beat*) What the fuck are you talking about?

JACK. I'm impotent.

KATIE. You're kidding?

JACK. You know what that means?

KATIE. In my line of work, I've run into it from time to time. (*beat*) I can help you.

JACK. You can't. It's dead. Totally, completely dead with no resurrection in sight. I haven't been good for years... years.

KATIE. (*innocently*) But what about the drugs they have, that Viagra stuff? I mean, that old guy can even throw a football through a tire.

JACK. I tried it.

KATIE. Did it help?

JACK. There are two side effects: stuffy nose and flushed face. I took the pill, and an hour later my face was as red as a fireman and I couldn't breathe. Even if I could, who wants to have sex in that condition?

KATIE. You should have told me.

JACK. I am telling you.

KATIE. You should have told me as soon as we met.

JACK. I couldn't.

KATIE. Why?

JACK. Because you would have run out the door. I didn't want you to leave before you got the chance to know me.

KATIE. I wouldn't have –

JACK. I didn't want you to leave before I had the chance to...to...love you.

KATIE. You love me?

JACK. Yes, I do.

(**KATIE** *has tears in her eyes.*)

KATIE. I want to see that ballet.

JACK. I thought we were staying in?

(*She hugs him.*)

What was that for?

KATIE. For being so kind when you knew you wouldn't be able to get anything from me. Just another reason why I love you.

(*She kisses his cheek and crosses to the bedroom door.*)

JACK. It's funny.

KATIE. What is?

JACK. For the last six months I thought I was teaching you. "By your students you'll be taught."

KATIE. What are you saying?

(**JACK** *opens his shirt revealing a crucifix.*)

I think I've been in a coma, too. (*beat*) You made me I want to wear this again.

(**KATIE** *hugs him.*)

JACK. I had a whole lifetime before I met you and now, it seems to have disappeared. I feel like you've been a part of me forever.

KATIE. It's just the beginning.

(**JACK** *takes a moment, a deep breath and then.*)

JACK. We need to have a serious talk when I get in next Friday.

KATIE. About what?

(*A moment.*)

JACK. Do you trust me?

KATIE. Of course.

JACK. First thing Friday evening. Everything has to be perfect. I'll make reservation for us at Cellini's.

KATIE. Pretty fancy.

JACK. Pretty important.

KATIE. This is going to drive me crazy all week. Can't you give me a hint?

(**JACK** *laughs*)

JACK. It's...a gift.

KATIE. Jack. I have everything I need, and *now*, everything I want.

JACK. Are you sure?

KATIE. What is it?

JACK. You're getting nuts. I promise you, the second the car pulls in front of Cellini's.

(**JACK** *hugs her.*)

KATIE. Okay. (*beat*) Will I like it?

(**KATIE** *extends her left arm behind Jack's back looking at her ring finger and smiling.*)

JACK. I'm counting on it.

KATIE. I'm more than what you made of me. I won't let you down.

(*She kisses him, turns, and excitedly exits to her bedroom.* **JACK** *crosses to the desk and pulls out a greeting card from the top drawer. He opens the colorful envelope and writes while gazing in the direction of Katie's guest room. After he is done he seals the envelope and places it on his desk. The lights slowly fade to black during this action.*)

Scene III

Setting: The same. Present time.

(*As the lights come up* **KATIE** *is in front of the guest bedroom door.*)

JULIA. Impotent? My Jack. The lumberjack! That's just isn't true.

KATIE. That's what he told me. (*beat*) He wasn't that way... with you?

(**JULIA** *shakes her head.*)

JULIA. Well it wasn't that often in the last year, but no, it was never a problem.

KATIE. Oh my God. This is crazy. He made such a point about it. He didn't want to tell me the truth until I fell in love with him.

JULIA. Why?

KATIE. He was afraid I would leave.

(**JULIA** *has a moment, then.*)

JULIA. Jack didn't want a lover; he wanted a little girl he could actually take outside and play with. Sarah couldn't do that.

KATIE. But there was Laura. Right?

(**JULIA** *is caught off guard.*)

JULIA. Yes, Laura. You're right.

(**JULIA** *crosses and looks out the window center stage.*)

KATIE. I never meant to hurt anyone.

(**KATIE** *turns and looks over the apartment.*)

It's hard to believe I won't be coming back here. (*beat*) Will you sell it now?

JULIA. I don't know. I didn't know he bought it until after he...died, three days ago. I'm not sure what I'll do with it.

KATIE. You should keep it. He loved it here.

JULIA. (*beat*) I know.

(**KATIE** *crosses to the guest bedroom, takes a moment, and then turns back to* **JULIA.**)

KATIE. How would *you* know he loved it here?

JULIA. He took me here once. About a year ago.

(*The lights go black.* **KATIE** *exits.* **JULIA** *remains. In the darkness the Carousel is removed, and* **KATIE'S** *picture is changed back to the picture that was removed in Act I Scene II. As the lights resume* **JACK** *enters from the apartment door. It is one year earlier.*)

JACK. What do you think?

JULIA. Impressive.

JACK. I knew you'd like it.

JULIA. I didn't say that. (*beat*) Jack, you didn't do something foolish, did you?

(**JACK** *behaves as a little boy caught with his hand in the cookie jar.*)

JACK. What?

JULIA. Don't tell me you bought this.

(**JACK** *doesn't answer.*)

You bought this apartment?

JACK. It's a perk of the firm, but...it could be more.

JULIA. Why would a Connecticut practice purchase an apartment in Manhattan?

JACK. It's a pied-á-terre.

JULIA. Excuse me?

JACK. French for, "foot on the ground." (*beat*) A second home. The partners do a lot of work in New York. It's nicer than staying at a hotel.

JULIA. Who does the sheets?

JACK. A maid, I guess.

(**JULIA** *explores the room. She examines the books closely.*)

JULIA. *A Tale of Two Cities, The Communist Manifesto, Wuthering Heights.* (*sarcastically*) Wow, that's fascinating.

(*She looks at* **JACK** *as she crosses to the piano.*)

A piano? Not a cello? Not a saxophone? (*beat*) A piano.

(*She turns and slyly smiles at him.*)

JACK. What?

JULIA. I was born at night, Jack...but it wasn't last night.

JACK. I don't know what you're –

JULIA. Lou certainly went out of his way to make you feel at home.

JACK. (*beat*) The partners all had a wish list.

JULIA. Uh huh.

JACK. It's great, isn't it?

JULIA. It's small.

JACK. Uncomplicated.

JULIA. Lonely.

JACK. A wonderful escape.

JULIA. Escape?

JACK. Yes.

JULIA. (*beat*) From Sarah?

JACK. No! Why would you say that?

JULIA. Because you were away a lot in her last few months.

JACK. A couple of days, every other week. You never said anything about it –

JULIA. I guess I didn't want to know what you were doing –

JACK. It was business, Julia...business, that's all. Was that so wrong? A little solace. A break from the constant nightmare –

JULIA. I never took a break.

JACK. You should have.

JULIA. Why are we here, Jack?

JACK. I wanted you to see where I've been staying.

JULIA. Very nice. Can we go home –

JACK. And to see what you might think about...living here.

JULIA. Live here? Are you crazy?

JACK. I could buy it from the firm. It would be a fresh start for us in a totally different environment. Away from –

(**JULIA** *starts to walk to the door.*)

JULIA. We have six thousand square feet on ten acres –

JACK. And we don't *have* to give it up. At least..not now. I'm only suggesting that we might spend more time here...together.

(**JULIA** *looks over the room.*)

JULIA. I couldn't fit the contents of my closet in this space. Let's go.

JACK. Wait, we just got here. Let me put on some music. I bought some wine. Please. Enjoy this. Kick off your shoes, unbutton something...if you want...relax.

(**JACK** *runs into the kitchen off stage.* **JULIA** *reluctantly sits on the couch, uncomfortable. She starts to take off her shoes then reconsiders and stops. She folds her arms across her chest.* **JACK** *enters. He turns on romantic music and places the glasses of wine on the table. He touches* **JULIA'S** *face.*)

Nice. This is nice.

JULIA. Yes.

(**JACK** *hands a glass to* **JULIA** *and lifts his glass in a toast.*)

JACK. Definitely a high point. "Without Utopias, life is nothing but a long and sad dress rehearsal for death." Serrat.

(*They drink.*)

Long time.

(**JULIA** *loosens a little.*)

JULIA. A very long time.

(**JACK** *gently touches her hair, sweeping it off her neck. He lovingly looks at her.*)

JACK. You're still the one person in this world that I enjoy being with more than anyone.

JULIA. Why?

JACK. Do I need a specific reason?

JULIA. If you're planning on getting me drunk tonight, you do.

(**JACK** *has a moment, then...*)

JACK. When we're at a cocktail party and I'm working the room, talking to clients, I can see you from the corner of my eye smiling at me. I know you know I'm lying, and I love it. (*beat*) I can call you sixteen times a day, and every time I talk to you it's like the first time. (*beat*) I love that you took such good care of my father and didn't fight with me to bring him into our home. (*beat*) Enough?

(**JULIA** *takes another sip of wine and* **JACK** *slowly leans in and kisses her.*)

JULIA. What else?

JACK. I have a gift for you!

(**JACK** *jumps up and crosses into the bedroom.*)

JULIA. I don't need anything.

JACK (O.S.). Close your eyes.

JULIA. Did you get me this or Susan?

JACK (O.S.). I did! Now close them.

(**JULIA** *closes her eyes.* **JACK** *enters, carrying the carousel. He places it on the coffee table in front of the couch.*)

JACK (CONT'D). Okay, open.

(**JULIA** *opens her eyes.*)

JULIA. Oh my God.

JACK. Happy Anniversary.

JULIA. It's not our anniversary.

JACK. Yes it is. Nineteen years ago. Central Park.

(**JULIA** *touches the carousel.*)

JULIA. It was hot as hell, and I didn't have money for the soda.

JACK. It was bottled water.

JULIA. You're right. You came out of nowhere and laid the money down.

JACK. Your knight in shining armor.

JULIA. Always. We rode this for over two hours.

JACK. I fell in love with you that day.

(**JACK** *turns the carousel on. The music plays as the horses move around.* **JULIA** *is obviously affected.*)

Better?

JULIA. Much better. You better hope we get divorced this year.

JACK. Why?

JULIA. You're going to have an *impossible* time topping this gift.

(**JACK** *smiles, leans in and gently kisses her. The kiss becomes deeper as* **JACK** *slowly removes her jacket. After a few moments* **JULIA** *gently pulls back from him.*)

JACK. What is it?

JULIA. I'm not sure I'm –

JACK. It's okay. Just relax.

(*He kisses her again but she slowly brings her hand up to her mouth. They remain clasped in each other's arms.*)

JULIA. I can't.

JACK. Please. Please. I'm doing the best I can. What do I need to do for you to love me again?

(*He leans in and kisses her again with more passion.* **JULIA** *tears.*)

JULIA. I don't know. Why don't you just give up on me?

JACK. I can't. I love you. You're worth fighting for.

JULIA. I don't feel that way.

JACK. Why? You've paid for the right to be happy. We both have.

JULIA. It hurts. I miss her so much, Jack.

JACK. She wouldn't have wanted it to destroy us. How much more are we going to allow this disease to ruin every facet of our lives? When do we say, enough? *Enough*, Julia! Please let me get close to you.

(**JULIA** *rises.*)

JULIA. Not yet.

JACK. When? She's been gone for a year.

JULIA. I *want* you to take me home now.

JACK. Julia –

JULIA. The problems are bigger than simply changing our address.

JACK. How many different ways can I say I'm sorry?

JULIA. Tell it to her.

JACK. I'm telling it to you. We played the odds.

JULIA. You played them.

JACK. It was a one in four chance. Jesus, you don't own this pain. She was my daughter, too!

JULIA. Was she? The nights I was alone with her. She must have seen the fear on my face because all she kept saying was, "it's okay, Mommy. I'm not scared."

(**JULIA** *cries.*)

JACK. Why didn't you tell me?

JULIA. Why weren't you there?

JACK. I was. As much as I could. I had important –

JULIA. Nothing was more important! Tell me!

JACK. Because I hated it! (*beat*) Because I'm not you. (*beat*) All I could do...was love her.

JULIA. I told you it would end like this.

JACK. Why do you despise me so much?

JULIA. Because you made me a believer. I went against my instincts, and I lost. Everything.

JACK. I don't know how much longer I can live like this. (*beat*) I wanted a child. I wanted you to be able to

feel...complete.
I thought a child would do that.

(**JACK** *picks up the carousel and places it back on the pedestal in the position of Act I Scene I.*)

JULIA. When are you going to stop trying to fix everything for me? Don't you think I wanted to dress my daughter up for her senior prom? Move her into the dorm? (*beat*) Help her pick out her wedding dress and watch you walk her down the aisle? But that wasn't to be. At least not with Sarah.

JACK. She's all we had.

JULIA. It was God's will.

JACK. No loving God could do this. Children are not supposed to predecease their parents.

JULIA. We never should have had her.

(*They reflect on their sadness in silence for a few moments.*)

JACK. It's funny, isn't it? At a party, I'm the guy that people want to be around. "I'm inspiring." I make them feel better about themselves. Rescue the world? I can't even save myself. All I can do is produce more damaged goods. I wanted children to grow and find real love. To be simply healthy and happy. I'm sorry I brought you into it. I'm a failure at the most simplest of chores...creating life beyond myself. That was my dream. Stupid, wasn't it?

(**JACK** *sits. There is an uncomfortable moment of silence as* **JULIA** *struggles within herself to make the most profound decision of her life.*)

JULIA. Jack...you will fulfill your dreams.

(*Lights come up on* **KATIE** *at the piano.* **KATIE** *crosses to the bookshelf and removes an envelope. She hands it to* **JULIA**.)

(*To* **KATIE**) What is this?

KATIE. (*To Julia*) There's about thirty-eight thousand dollars there.

JULIA. (*To* **KATIE**) I don't understand.

KATIE. (*To* **JULIA**) Jack gave me what I needed. After the first month I didn't come here for the money.

JULIA. (*To* **KATIE**) You should take it. I'm sure you can use it.

(**JULIA** *doesn't take the envelope.*)

KATIE. (*To* **JULIA**) I don't want it.

(**KATIE** *drops it on the coffee table, crosses and sits at the piano.*)

JULIA. (*To* **KATIE**) Where will you go?

KATIE. (*To* **JULIA**) I don't know. I really cared about him, you know. Now I see so did you. I'm very sorry, Julia.

JULIA. (*To* **KATIE**) Your parents really missed out.

(**KATIE** *shakes her head and sits. She pushes on the keys.*)

(*To* **KATIE**) What's wrong?

KATIE. (*To* **JULIA**) I never really thought about them until I left home. It must be my fault, right? What's the point of looking for them?

The first time I was a bundle of hope, now I'm a teenage hooker. I don't have a lot to offer them.

JULIA. (*To* **KATIE**) (*beat*) Katie, what are you telling me?

JACK. (*To* **JULIA**) How am I going to fulfill my dreams?

(*A moment.*)

JULIA. (*To* **JACK**) (*beat*) I got pregnant in 1987.

JACK. (*To* **JULIA**) What are you talking about? We were together in 1987.

JULIA. (*To* **JACK**) I broke up with you in early December.

JACK. (*To* **JULIA**) Yes. You told me you didn't love me anymore.

JULIA. (*To* **JACK**) I lied.

KATIE. (*Strongly to* **JULIA**) Why did they do it? (*beat*) I can't think of *any excuse* that would have made it okay for my real parents to dump me with a bunch of nuns –

JULIA. (*To* **KATIE**) Oh sweet Jesus, this is not happening.

KATIE. (*To* **JULIA**) What is going on?

JULIA. (*To* **KATIE**) He didn't have sex with you because he was impotent! He *couldn't* have sex with you!

JACK. (*To* **JULIA**) Why?

JULIA. (*To* **JACK**) I knew you would never accept my decision.

JACK. (*To* **JULIA**) Whose child was it? (*beat*) Julia, *who* was the father?

JULIA. (*To* **JACK**) You.

JACK. (*To* **JULIA**) Me?

JULIA. (*To* **JACK**) When I found out, I panicked. I knew you would want to keep it so I broke up with you. I couldn't go through the hell of having another person I loved die in my arms. I couldn't take the risk.

KATIE. (*To* **JULIA**) What are you saying?

JULIA. (*To* **KATIE**) You were wrong when you said a parent would have no excuse to give up a child. There are good reasons. Like a mother who carries a child who she is certain won't see her sixteenth birthday. A mother who isn't strong enough to take her unborn child's life but can't accept and watch God take that child away from her slowly, a little more each day. A mother whose worse day of her life was (*beat*) September 28, 1988.

(**KATIE** *looks at her and puts it all together.*)

KATIE. (*To* **JULIA**) That's my...birthday.

JULIA. (*To* **KATIE**) I know.

JACK. (*To* **JULIA**) You had an abortion?

JULIA. (*To* **JACK**) No! My God, no! You know I could never do that. *You* made my choice.

JACK. (*To* **JULIA**) I did? I didn't even –

JULIA. (*To* **JACK**) You always told me how lucky you were to be adopted. That your parents were the greatest. I hid the pregnancy and I signed up with Catholic Charities. When the baby was born, I never saw her. The sisters took her, and I left. I had no idea where she went.

Laura is nineteen now.

JACK. (*To* **JULIA**) Laura?

JULIA. (*To* **JACK**) I gave her my sister's name. I thought she would like that.

JACK. (*To* **JULIA**) I have another daughter?

KATIE. (*To* **JULIA**) Oh my God. I'm going to be sick.

JACK. (*To* **JULIA**) I called you every day for a month just to be ignored. Why *did* you call me again?

JULIA. (*To* **JACK**) Because that year without you was the worst year of my life. It was like a year without breathing.

JACK. (*To* **JULIA**) Why are you telling me this now?

JULIA. (*To* **JACK**) Because you have a child! You're not a failure.

KATIE. (*To* **JULIA**) You're my mother?

(**JULIA** *nods.*)

(*To* **JULIA**) Jack is my father?

(**JULIA** *nods.*)

JACK. (*To* **JULIA**) Do you know her?

JULIA. (*To* **JACK**) Yes. Every detail.

KATIE. (*To* **JULIA**) Oh my God. I thought he was going to ask me to marry him this weekend. Oh my God! Are you my gift? Are you my gift?

JACK. (*To* **JULIA**) Then you've met her? You've seen her?

(**JULIA** *is desperate in her desire to believe her fantasies.*)

JULIA. (*To* **JACK**) I've watched her grow up. I've seen her running through the grass and playing with the other children. I've seen her riding ponies, and laughing on the roller coaster. Playing make believe with her friends and going shopping with her mother.

JACK. (*To* **JULIA**) Where does she live?

JULIA. (*To* **JACK**) She's in her first year at Stanford. Her parents were busting with pride when she graduated valedictorian. And what a high school career. Head cheerleader, honor society. She's been loved and cherished as the most sought after prize in the world. You see, that's how couples treat adopted kids. Her parents are wealthy and they've given her the best of everything.

KATIE. (*To* **JULIA**) I'm Laura, aren't I? Your fantasy daughter! Tell me! I'm Laura.

(**JULIA** *doesn't react.*)

(*To* **JULIA**) The perfect student, the apple of her mother's eye?

JULIA. (*To* **JACK**) She's not only book smart, but she's people smart. Everyone wants to be her friend. And she's *healthy*, really healthy. She doesn't have a worry in the world. She asks about us all the time. She can't wait to meet us one day.

(**JACK** *grabs her.*)

JACK. (*To* **JULIA**) Julia, look at me. Look at me. You don't really know these things, do you?

JULIA. (*To* **JACK**) I do. Laura is in her first year at –

JACK. (*To* **JULIA**) Laura could be as dead as –

JULIA. (*To* **JACK**) No, don't say that. I couldn't stand...She's out there and she's happy.

KATIE. (*To* **JULIA**) Disappointed, mommy? Your imaginary little princess is a whore.

(**KATIE** *cries and runs off.*)

JULIA. (*To* **JACK**) Every time I looked at Sarah lying there, I thought of Laura running and playing. Don't you see, I'm right. I've got to be, and I won't consider anything else.

(**JACK** *backs away from her.*)

JACK. (*To* **JULIA**) How could you throw my daughter away without even talking to me?

JULIA. (*To* **JACK**) The pregnancy came too soon for me. The horror of my sister was still very real in my mind.

JACK. (*To* **JULIA**) I lost a brother...to that same disease.

JULIA. (*To* **JACK**) But you *weren't* responsible. He didn't depend on you. You went out with your friends. Parties, proms. Danny's illness didn't slow you down. (*beat*) He didn't die in *your* arms.

JACK. (*To* **JULIA**) Am I supposed to feel guilty for living my life?

JULIA. (*To* **JACK**) I did. Laura was my twin. How could I enjoy myself when my sister couldn't breathe? I couldn't risk going through all of that again...this time with my own child.

(*A moment*)

JACK. (*To* **JULIA**) How could you do this and not look back?

JULIA. (*To* **JACK**) Not a day went by that I didn't think of her. The years of sleepless nights wondering is she sick? Did she inherit our legacy? (*beat*) Did I give her away for nothing? Did I sentence an innocent couple who loves this child to misery? Does she look like us? Does she wonder who I am and why I gave her up? How could Jack ever forgive me? Could I ever forgive myself?

JACK. (*To* **JULIA**) Why didn't you ever tell me?

JULIA. (*To* **JACK**) Because you would have wanted to look for her.

JACK. (*To* **JULIA**) I'm going to find her.

JULIA. (*To* **JACK**) You can't!

JACK. (*To* **JULIA**) I need to! You want me to!

JULIA. (*To* **JACK**) How?

JACK. (*To* **JULIA**) I'm a partner in the largest law firm in Connecticut. We use private investigators every day.

JULIA. (*To* **JACK**) But we don't even know what state she's in.

JACK. (*To* **JULIA**) Computers. Internet. The world has become a small place, Julia. I will find her.

JULIA. (*To* **JACK**) She may not even know she's adopted. Maybe she's happy. She hasn't come looking for us.

JACK. (*To* JULIA) I'm her father. I want her to know that. I need to know my daughter!

JULIA. (*To* JACK) Maybe she doesn't need to know you. Are you thinking of that? Even if you can find her, what makes you think she'll fall into your arms?

JACK. (*To* JULIA) I'll take that chance. I'll get her to know us before I tell her.

JULIA. (*To* JACK) What if you find out the worst?

JACK. (*To* JULIA) I'll deal with it.

(*To* JULIA) I'm willing to accept whoever she is or isn't and whatever the consequences are. We need to be sure. This may be our last chance. Don't you want to know?

(*A moment, then* JULIA *mentally retreats.*)

(*To* JULIA) Julia. Don't you want to know?

JULIA. (*To* JACK) I do know. Laura is in her first year at Stanford –

JACK. (*To* JULIA) No Julia, stop –

JULIA. (*To* JACK) Her parents were busting with pride when she graduated valedictorian –

JACK. (*To* JULIA) Stop it! Stop it! Stop it!

(JACK *shakes her and then quits.* JULIA *screams.*)

JULIA. (*To* JACK) No! I couldn't bear it. (*pause*) This is all the faith that I have. It can't be any other way. Promise me you'll never look.

(*A moment. She looks into* JACK'S *eyes.*)

(*To* JULIA) Jack. Love me enough to make this the truth. Please. Give me your word.

(*He reluctantly acquiesces to her.* JULIA *smiles at him, crosses to the couch, and sits.* JULIA *temporarily has lost touch with reality.*)

(*To* JACK) Jack. (*pause*) Tell me about our daughter.

JACK. (*To* JULIA) What?

(JACK *understands and realizes that he has lost her for*

the moment. He supports her.)

(*To* JULIA) She's beautiful, just like her mother.

(**JACK** *crosses and kneels behind the couch, placing his arms around her.*)

JULIA. (*To* JACK) Is she nice? Friendly?

JACK. (*To* JULIA) Very friendly. Everyone loves her. She's going to school to be a lawyer, like her dad.

(**KATIE** *enters the room.*)

KATIE. (*To* JULIA) I can't believe you did this to me. Do you have any idea what you sentenced me to?

JACK. (*To* JULIA) She can also play the piano, and in her spare time, she reads all the great literature.

JULIA. (*To* KATIE) Yes...I do.

KATIE. (*To* JULIA) No, you don't. Night after night, alcohol breathing on my neck as they push themselves inside me. Closing my eyes and going anywhere else in the world for that fifteen minutes.

JACK. (*To* JULIA) She's really good to her adoptive parents and she thinks about us all the time.

(*To* JULIA) And when she's ready, she's going to find us and we're going to be able to tell her all about her real family. She doesn't blame you, and she loves you.

(*During this speech* **JACK** *picks up the wine glasses and exits toward the kitchen.*)

JULIA. (*To* JACK) You see. Isn't this better. Please let it stay this way. Promise me.

(*The lights go to black as and Katie's picture is returned to the wall.*)

(*To* KATIE) I'm sorry.

KATIE. Not accepted.

(**KATIE** *angrily crosses to the coffee table and picks up the envelope with the money. She turns to leave, but is stopped by the picture she bought for Jack.* **KATIE** *takes the bills from the envelope and throws them at the picture.*)

Lying bastard. I hate you. I fucking hate you. I don't need you.

(**KATIE** *turns on* **JULIA**.)

And I don't need you! Get the hell out of my way!

JULIA. Please. Katie, it's too late for Jack and me. I've lost the chance to tell him how sorry I am...for everything. For blaming him for Sarah. For making him lose out on nineteen precious years with his daughter.

KATIE. I don't feel sorry for you. He lied to me.

JULIA. He wanted to rescue you.

KATIE. I'm sorry I couldn't live up to Laura. I'm sorry he was embarrassed by me.

JULIA. He would never be embarrassed by his child.

KATIE. What a crock of shit.

JULIA. You can't blame him. He only tried to make it right.

KATIE. It doesn't matter.

JULIA. I don't want to lose you again.

KATIE. You never had me...and I never had you.

JULIA. You can now!

KATIE. This is *your* place. I need five minutes to get my things, and I'll be out of here.

(**KATIE** *turns to enter the guest room but then stops and looks at* **JULIA**.)

There's one thing I never understood. (*beat*) At the end of every weekend Jack would always kiss me goodbye and out of the corner of my eye I saw him tasting his lips. Why?

JULIA. He was making sure.

KATIE. Of what?

JULIA. Children with Cystic Fibrosis have a high amount of salt in their sweat.

KATIE. Oh Jesus. Too much information. Have a nice life.

JULIA. Katie, please.

(**KATIE** *turns to enter the guest room but pauses and*

leans her head against the door.)

KATIE. (*beat*) I miss him.

JULIA. So do I.

(**KATIE** *shakes her head resisting the moment.*)

KATIE. It's not enough.

JULIA. Jack spent six months setting up this day for the two of us. To make us a family. If you walk out that door right now, it will all go away.

(**KATIE** *enters the guest room.*)

Where are you going?

KATIE (O.S.). Anywhere I can just be who I am.

JULIA. You can do that...right here.

(**KATIE** *sticks her head into the room.*)

KATIE. Yeah right. As long as I keep a thesaurus up my ass and don't touch the frickin' precious carousel, I should be perfect.

JULIA. Jack was wrong. I would have accepted you in any condition. (**JULIA** *takes a deep breath*) You're my daughter.

(*A moment*)

KATIE. I could never trust you.

JULIA. Just give me a chance.

KATIE. You had it. Nineteen years ago.

(**KATIE** *enters the guest bedroom.* **JULIA**, *wounded, crosses to the desk to retrieve her pocketbook. She again notices the greeting card that* **JACK** *left in Act II Scene II that she began to open in Act I Scene I. She cautiously opens it and reads it. She sits and softly cries. After several moments* **KATIE** *enters with a packed suitcase. She crosses to the door.*)

(*sarcastically*) Don't be a stranger, mom. I'll write you from Stanford.

JULIA. Katie.

(**JULIA** *rises with card in hand.*)

KATIE. What is it?

JULIA. A card from Jack.

(**KATIE** *puts her suitcase down and quickly crosses to the desk.*)

KATIE. Let me have it!

(**KATIE** *reaches for the card.*)

JULIA. It was...for me.

KATIE. (*to herself*) Of course it is.

(**KATIE** *turns and crosses to the door.* **JULIA** *reads from the card.*)

JULIA. Dear Julia. Happy Anniversary. You have every right to be angry with me. I lied to you. But it's not you that I feel disloyal to tonight. I promised her a gift but it's not what she expects but what I hope she desperately wants.

(**KATIE** *hesitates at the door.*)

It is also a gift to you. One which defines the love I have for you and always will. (*beat*) She's beautiful, inside and out. I hope you can love her as much as I do. It was easy for me. (*beat*) She is you. Jack.

(*The lights go to black as* **KATIE** *turns towards* **JULIA**.)

THE END

TIME LINE OF PIED-À-TERRE

June 1987 - Jack 31, attorney, meets Julia, age 25 (graduate student) at Central Park picnic for Cystic Fibrosis.

December 1987 – Julia becomes pregnant after dating Jack six months.

Mid December 1987 - Julia panics, hides pregnancy, breaks up with Jack.

September 28, 1988 – Julia gives birth to Katie and gives her up for adoption.

January 1989 - Julia re-contacts Jack and their relationship rekindles. (After a one year break up)

May 1990 - Jack and Julia marry.

1992 – Sarah is born.

April 2005 - Jack buys apartment in NYC unknown to Julia. Spends several weekends a month in New York City working.

June 2005 - Sarah dies at age 13.

Jack continues his work in NYC apartment till **June 2006** when he first brings Julia there. One year after the death of Sarah.

June 2006 – Julia and Jack celebrate 19 year anniversary of Central Park meeting.

June 2006 -Jack learns of Katie existence.

July 2006 – Jack hires a private investigator to locate Katie.

December 2006 – Jack learns that Katie is alive.

January 2007 - Jack brings Katie to his apartment for the first time.

June 2007 – Jack plans to introduce Katie to Julia on their 20 anniversary of their Central Park meeting

PROP LIST

Katie's Painting	**KATIE**	Living Room
Carousel	**JULIA**	Living Room
Telephone		On the Desk
Intercom		On kitchen shelf
Small Recorder	**JACK**	On the Desk
Headphones	**KATIE**	Enters w/ it (Outside)
Shopping bag from Victoria Secrets	**KATIE**	Enters w/ it (Outside)
Purse	**KATIE**	Enters w/ it (Outside)
Purse	**JULIA**	On her person
Tissues	**JACK**	On the Desk behind lamp
Cuff link box	**JACK**	On the Desk
ABT Playbill	**JACK**	On his person
Laptop	**JACK**	On the Desk
Pack of Gum	**KATIE**	In her purse
Negligee and matching panties	**KATIE**	In Vicky Bag
Keys	**JULIA**	On her person
Keys	**KATIE**	On her person
Tums	**KATIE**	Kitchen
Sheet Music	**JACK/JULIA**	On the Piano
Other Painting		Other side of the Wall
Purse	**KATIE**	Enters w/ it (Outside)
Glass with "7-Up"	**JACK**	Living Room
Ashtray	**JACK**	On Table
$100.00 bill	**KATIE**	Maybe in purse or pocket
Pencils and Pens	**JACK**	On or in the desk
Papers, Portfolios, etc.	**JACK**	On or in the desk
Portfolio	**JACK**	Backstage
Biology Book	**KATIE**	Kitchen
Notebook	**KATIE**	Kitchen
Chess Pieces and Board: King, Queen, and 4 Pawns	**JACK**	On the side table
Mug	**JACK**	On the desk
Wallet	**JACK**	On or in the desk

Car Registration	**JULIA**	In her wallet
"Laura's" Picture	**JULIA**	In her wallet
Cell Phone	**KATIE**	Backstage
Cell Phone	**JULIA**	Her purse
Travel Pack of Tissues	**JULIA**	Her purse
Newspaper Clipping	**JULIA**	Her purse
Sword	**JACK**	His bedroom
Stereo / Boom box	**JACK**	Living Room
Stereo / Boom box Remote	**JACK**	Living Room
Greeting Card w/ Envelope	**JACK**	In the desk
2x Filled Glasses of Wine	**JACK**	Kitchen
Gift Box for the Carousel	**JACK**	His bedroom
Envelope w/ $38,000	**KATIE**	Backstage
Two Packed "Bags"	**KATIE**	Her bedroom

FURNITURE:

Piano	**JACK**	USC
Chair		USL Corner (2nd Level)
Carpet		DSC
Desk w/ Chair	**JACK**	DSR
Bookshelf	**JACK**	CR
Console	**JACK**	USR (1st Level)
Sofa	**JACK**	Center Right
Table / Side Table	**JACK**	Center Left
Armchair	**JACK**	DSC Left
Pedestal	**JACK**	DSL
Coffee Table	**JACK**	DSC
Desk lamp	**JACK**	SR
Piano Lamp	**JACK**	USC (2nd Level)
Floor Lamp	**JACK**	USL Corner (2nd Level)

PERISHABLES:

2x Filled Glasses of Wine	**JACK**	Kitchen
Greeting Card w/ Envelope	**JACK**	In the desk
Travel Pack of Tissues	**JULIA**	Her purse
Pack of Gum	**KATIE**	In her pant pocket
Tissues		Living Room
Tums	**KATIE**	Kitchen
Glass with "7-Up"	**JACK**	Living Room

COSTUME PLOT

Costume Designer: Brad L. Scoggins
Original Costume Design, Copyright © 2007 by Brad L. Scoggins
All Rights Reserved (Reprinted by permission)

JULIA

WORN THROUGHOUT:
Nude Bra
Off-White, Long-Sleeved Silk Charmeuse Blouse
Off-White/Tan/Light Green Linen Pencil Skirt
Off-White, Lightweight, Crepe Coat
    w/Teal Patterned Chiffon Scarf, worn under collar & lapel
Pewter 'Designer' Heels
Rhinestone & Gold Clip-On Earrings
Gold Chain Necklace w/Rhinestone & Gold Pendant
Gold Watch
Gold w/Rhinestone Wedding Band
Gold w/White "Diamond" Engagement Ring
Tan Leather 'Designer' Purse
    w/Pewter Leather Wallet, containing:
        Photo(s) of "Laura"
        Car Registration
    Newspaper 'Obituary' Clipping
    "Jack's" Cell Phone

ACT I, SCENE 3:
REPEAT: All

ACT II, SCENE 1:
REPEAT: All

ACT II, SCENE 3:
REPEAT: All for Top of Scene

DURING SCENE, ONSTAGE:
(*JACK: "Wait, we just got here. Let me put on some Music..."*):
LOSE:
Coat w/Scarf
    (Jack assists; takes Coat & Scarf offstage)

KATIE

WORN THROUGHOUT:
Charcoal Grey Leggings w/Lace Trim
Gold Necklace w/Crucifix

ACT I, SCENE 1:
Hot Pink, Lace-Trimmed Bra (Worn Throughout ACT I)
Hot Pink Cotton Tank Top
Men's Tangerine & White Striped Dress Shirt (Jack's Dress Shirt from Act II, Scene 2); (Worn as Mini-Dress; Slightly wrinkled, Sleeves Rolled-Up)
Plum Metallic Wide Belt w/Gold Buckle
Green w/Pink, Orange & Yellow Striped Socks
Green & Purple, Loosely-Woven, Long Scarf
    (Worn as Headband)
Gold w/Purple Gemstone 'Dangly' Earrings
Yellow & Orange 'Skrunchie', worn on Wrist
Multi-Colored, Patterned Rubber Boots
Large, Orange & White, Leather 'Designer' Purse
    Preset w/:
    Pink Gum in Package
    Cell Phone
    'Vintage' Coin Purse/Wallet
    Earphones/MP3 Player
    Keys on Decorative Keychain

DURING SCENE, ONSTAGE:
LOSE, Upon Entrance:
Rubber Boots

(KATIE: "Tonight…tonight. It's so exciting. He's giving me a gift…")
LOSE:
Scarf, Earrings

(KATIE: "…I have to make this happen. He's ready and I'm so ready I'm going to burst."
LOSE:
Belt

ACT I, SCENE 2:
REPEAT:
Bra, Leggings, Green Striped Socks; Gold Necklace w/Crucifix

LOSE:
'Jack's' Dress Shirt, Pink Tank Top, Yellow & Orange 'Skrunchie' on Wrist

ADD:

Black w/Red Metallic Print, Stretch Velvet Short Shorts
Green/Lavender/Burnt Orange Patterned Halter Top
Burnt Orange, Zip-Front Sweater w/Fur Trimmed Hood
Antique Gold 'Pleather', Zip-Front Jacket
    w/Multi-Colored, Sequin & Rhinestone Flower Brooch
    w/Packaged Condom in small outside Pocket
Green & Purple, Losely-Woven Scarf (REPEAT)
    Worn wrapped around Neck
Purple Ankle Boots
Multi-Colored, Striped Leg Warmers
Large, Gold 'Dangly' Earrings
Gold Necklace w/Crucifix (REPEAT)
Gold & Purple Gemstone Bracelet
Multi-Colored, Rhinestone Hairclip
Oversized, Multicolored, 'Ethnic' Patchwork Shoulder Bag
    Preset w/:
        'Vintage' Coin Purse/Wallet
        w/$100 Bill
    Misc. Clothing, Accessories

DURING SCENE, ONSTAGE:
(JACK: "...Pop had this talent of peeling an apple in one continuous piece...")
LOSE:
Scarf around Neck (Tie onto Strap of Shoulder Bag)

*(***KATIE***: "Hey, my name ain't Serena, it's Katie."*
LOSE:
Earrings

ACT I, SCENE 3:
REPEAT:
Bra, Leggings, Green Striped Socks; Gold Necklace w/Crucifix

LOSE:
Gold 'Pleather' Jacket, Hooded Sweater, Halter Top, Shorts, Leg Warmers, Boots, Hairclip, Bracelet

ADD:
Pink Tank Top
'Jack's' Dress Shirt
Yellow & Orange 'Skrunchie' on Wrist

ACT I, SCENE 4:
REPEAT:
Bra, Leggings, Pink Tank Top, Green Striped Socks; Gold Necklace w/Crucifix

LOSE:

'Jack's' Dress Shirt, 'Skrunchie' on Wrist

OVERDRESS:
Orange Cotton Tank Top w/Lace Trim
Orange w/Green & Pink Polka-Dot Socks

ADD:
Pink & White Striped Pajama Bottoms
Blue, Pleat-Front, Tailored, Collarless Cotton Blouse w/White Neckband
    Worn Open, Unbuttoned & Untucked
Hot Pink 'Skrunchie' in Hair, worn in 80's-Style Pony Tail

DURING SCENE, ONSTAGE:
(**KATIE**: *"A Fucking Snob."*)
LOSE:
Blue Tailored Blouse

DURING SCENE, ONSTAGE:
(**KATIE**: *"Just admit it…you're a fucking snob."*)
RE-ENTER, ADDING:
Oversized Purple Sweater

DURING SCENE, OFFSTAGE:
(**KATIE**: *"Because experiencing it is what's fun…"*)
LOSE:
Orange w/Green & Pink Polka Dot Socks

ADD:
Light Tan, Knee-Length, Quilted Winter Coat w/Fur-Trimmed Hood
    Preset w/Green & Purple Scarf in Left Outer Pocket
    Preset w/Multi-Colored Knitted Winter Cap & Fingerless Gloves in
    Right Outer Pocket
Tan, 'Ugg'-Style Boots

DURING SCENE, ONSTAGE:
(**KATIE**: *"Out. Out with the poor people.)*
ADD:
Green & Purple Scarf
    Worn wrapped around Neck

DURING SCENE, ONSTAGE:
(**KATIE**: *"And I'm sick of it. You're suffocating me…"*)
LOSE:
Pink 'Skrunchie'

ADD:
Multi-Colored, Knitted Cap
Multi-Colored, Fingerless Gloves

(**JACK**: *"You're burning up…"*)
LOSE: Cap, Scarf

(**JACK**: *"I'm calling 911. We need an ambulance."*)

LOSE: Coat, Gloves

ACT I, SCENE 5:
REPEAT:

Bra, Leggings, Pink Tank Top, Green Striped Socks; Gold Necklace w/ Crucifix

LOSE:

Sweater, Orange Tank Top, 'Ugg' Boots, Pajama Bottoms

ADD:

'Jack's' Dress Shirt
Yellow & Orange 'Skrunchie' on Wrist

ACT II, SCENE 1:
LOSE:

Pink Bra

ADD:

Periwinkle Blue, Camisole-Strapped Leotard (Worn Throughout Act II)

REPEAT:

Leggings, Gold Necklace w/Crucifix; Pink Tank Top, 'Jack's' Dress Shirt, Green Striped Socks,
Yellow & Orange 'Skrunchie' on Wrist

ACT II, SCENE 2:
REPEAT:

Blue Leotard, Leggings, Gold Necklace w/Crucifix

LOSE:

Pink Tank Top, 'Jack's' Dress Shirt, Green Striped Socks, Yellow & Orange 'Skrunchie' on Wrist

ADD:

Teal Chiffon 'Ballet' Rehearsal Skirt
Slate Blue Leg Warmers w/Buttons
Purple Iridescent, Beaded 'Skrunchie'; Hair in 'Ballet' bun

ACT II, SCENE 3:
REPEAT:

Leotard, Leggings; Gold Necklace w/Crucifix

LOSE:

Chiffon Skirt, Leg Warmers, Beaded 'Skrunchie'

ADD:

'Jack's' Dress Shirt
Green Striped Socks
Yellow & Orange 'Skrunchie' on Wrist

DURING SCENE, ONSTAGE:

(**KATIE**: *"Oh my God. I thought he was going to ask me to marry him this weekend…"*)

PARTIALLY UNBUTTON:
'Jack's' Dress Shirt

DURING SCENE, OFFSTAGE:
LOSE:
'Jack's' Dress Shirt, Pink Tank Top, Green Striped Socks, Yellow & Orange 'Skrunchie'

ADD:

Orange Tank Top w/Lace Trim (REPEAT from ACT I, SCENE 4)
Blue Denim Jeans
Blue, Pleat-Front, Tailored, Collarless Cotton Blouse w/White Neckband (REPEAT from ACT I, SCENE 4)
    Worn Buttoned, Untucked
Wide Leather, Pewter-Colored Belt
    Worn over Blouse
Brown Leather, Sandal-Style Heels
Large Gold Hoop Earrings
Brown Tortoise-Shell Hairband

DURING SCENE:
(**KATIE**: *"Don't be a stranger, Mom. I'll write you from Stanford."*)
RE-ENTER, Carrying:
Oversized, Multicolored, 'Ethnic' Patchwork Shoulder Bag
    'Packed' w/
        Purple Sweater (from ACT I, SCENE 4)
        Teal Chiffon Skirt (from ACT II, SCENE 2)
        Misc. Clothing
Green & Purple Scarf, tied around strap of bag

JACK

WORN THROUGHOUT:
White Crew-Neck T-Shirt, Gold Watch

ACT I, SCENE 2:
White, Point-Collared, Pleat-Front 'Tux' Shirt
    w/Black & Gold 'Stud' Buttons
    w/Black & Gold Cufflinks
Black 'Tux' Pants
    w/Black Suspenders
Black Bow Tie
Black Cummerbund
Black Tuxedo Jacket
Tan Socks
Black, Patent-Leather, Formal Shoes

OVERDRESS:
Tall Black Socks

DURING SCENE, ONSTAGE:
(**JACK**: *"I need to get out of this 'bird suit'. Make yourself comfortable."*)
LOSE:
Cufflinks

DURING SCENE, OFFSTAGE:
REPEAT:
White T-Shirt, Tan Socks

LOSE:
Jacket, Bow Tie, Cummerbund, 'Tux' Shirt, Pants, Black Shoes, Black Socks

ADD:
Dark Aqua, Point-Collared Dress Shirt
Dark Tan, Pleated Slacks
    w/Brown Braided Leather Belt
Brown Leather Loafers

DURING SCENE, ONSTAGE:
(*After Katie's exit*)
ADD:
Gold, Wire-Rimmed Reading Glasses (Preset on Piano at Top of Show)

ACT I, SCENE 4:
REPEAT:
White T-Shirt, Tan Socks, Dark Tan Pleated Slacks w/Braided Leather Belt, Brown Leather Shoes,
Gold Watch, Reading Glasses

LOSE:
Dark Aqua Dress Shirt

ADD:
Royal Blue & Teal Plaid, Point-Collared Dress Shirt
Olive Green, V-Neck 'Cashmere' Sweater

ACT II, SCENE 2:
REPEAT:
White T-Shirt, Gold Watch

LOSE:
Green Sweater, Blue & Green Plaid Shirt, Dark Tan Pleated Slacks w/ Braided Belt, Tan Socks

ADD:
Black Opaque Tights (Worn Throughout ACT II)
Off-White 'Poet's' Shirt w/Ruffle at Collar & Cuffs
Oversized Burgundy w/Black & Gold Pumpkin Breeches w/Black Elastic Suspenders
Black Leather Slippers
Pewter-Colored 16th Century Breastplate
Black Velvet Capelet w/Burgundy & Gold Brocade Lining
Pewter-Colored, 16th Century Helmet
Dark Brown, Curled Moustache & Goatee
Gold Chain w/Crucifix

DURING SCENE, ONSTAGE:
LOSE:
(Katie Removes) Helmet, Goatee, Capelet, Breastplate

(**KATIE**: *"Now we're ready to seriously practice."*)
Katie Drops Jack's Suspenders, allowing Breeches to fall to the floor

DURING SCENE, OFFSTAGE:
(**JACK**: *"Now I feel like an idiot and…!"*)
LOSE:
Breeches, Poet's Shirt

ADD:
Taupe & Grey Silk Robe w/Self Belt

DURING SCENE, OFFSTAGE:
(**JACK**: *"I've got to change. We have dinner in two hours and then the ballet."*)
LOSE:
Robe, Slippers

ADD:
Tangerine & White Striped Dress Shirt
Light Khaki, Flat-Front, Cotton Twill Pants
  w/Oxblood Leather Belt

Lightweight, Tan Plaid Blazer
Taupe Socks
Oxblood, Wing-Tip Loafers

BRING ON:
Yellow w/Orange Printed Tie (Never Worn)

DURING SCENE, ONSTAGE:
(*After Katie's exit*)
ADD:
Reading Glasses

ACT II, SCENE 3:
REPEAT:
White T-Shirt, Black Tights, Taupe Socks, Oxblood Wing-Tip Loafers, Gold Watch, Gold Chain w/Crucifix

LOSE:
Tan Blazer, Khaki Pants, Tangerine & White Striped Shirt

ADD:

White, Point-Collared Dress Shirt
    Worn w/Top Button Unbuttoned
Burnt Orange & Grey Striped Tie
    Cinched Loosely around Neck
Charcoal Grey Suit Trousers
    w/Grey Patterned Suspenders
Charcoal Grey Suit Jacket

SOUND PLOT

Design by Chris Rummel

ACT 1

Scene I
Carousel music plays after Julia winds it.
Apartment telephone rings.
Jack's voice on personal recorder (VO).

Scene II
Beethoven's Opus 28.

Scene III
Apartment telephone rings (continue through transition into Act I Scene IV).

Scene IV
Apartment telephone rings.
Door Buzzer.

Scene V
Jack's cell phone rings.

ACT 2

Scene II
Jack's cell phone rings.
Ballet music from stereo.

Scene III
Romantic mood music.
Carousel music.

SET DESIGN

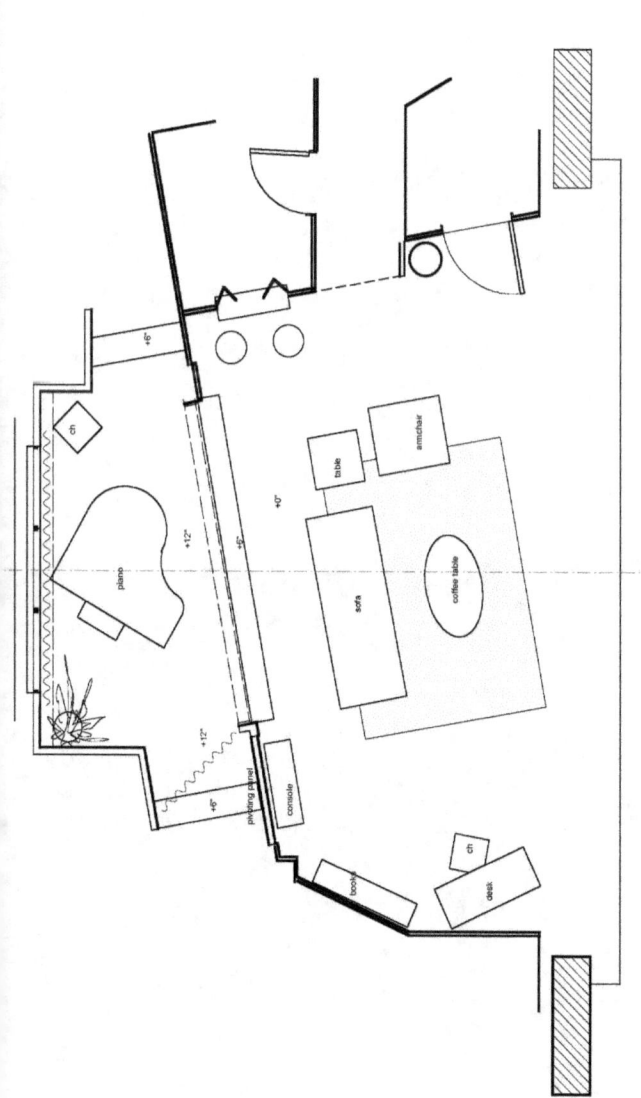

www.ingramcontent.com/pod-product-compliance
Lightning Source LLC
Chambersburg PA
CBHW070646300426
44111CB00013B/2281